WHAT ON EARTH IS THIS KINGDOM?

What On Earth Is This Kingdom?

GERALD COATES

KINGSWAY PUBLICATIONS
EASTBOURNE

Unless otherwise indicated, Scripture quotations
are from the New American Standard Bible,
© The Lockman Foundation 1960, 1962, 1963, 1968,
1971, 1972, 1973.

RSV = Revised Standard Version
      copyright 1946, 1952, © 1971, 1973 by the
      Division of Christian Education of the
      National Council of the Churches
      of Christ in the USA

TLB = The Living Bible
      © Tyndale House Publishers 1971

AV = Authorized Version (crown copyright)

NIV = New International Version
      © New York International Bible Society 1978

Printed in Great Britain for
KINGSWAY PUBLICATIONS LTD
Lottbridge Drove, Eastbourne, E. Sussex BN23 6NT by
Richard Clay (The Chaucer Press) Ltd, Bungay, Suffolk.
Typeset by Nuprint Services Ltd, Harpenden, Herts.

Contents

All the stories and accounts in this book are true. Some names of people and places have been changed, to protect the innocent and the guilty!

With Thanks

How do you thank the growing number of people God uses to shape and influence your life? I remember Hugh Good and Mr Jeffries who led me to Christ while a boy. 'Old' Mr West and Mr Fellows whose enthusiasm and love for Jesus and the Scriptures kept me on course in my days with the Brethren.

I'm extremely grateful to God for the impact of the lives of Nigel Goodwin, Doug Barnett and Roger Forster. They helped shape my thinking, enabling me to be more an 'original' than a 'copy'.

I shall always be in the debt of Maurice Smith for taking me under his wing fifteen years ago—yet never wanting to possess me. He continually made room for me at meetings and conferences but especially in his relationships and friendships with others. Then there is John Noble, to whom I have looked for so much help, advice, encouragement and correction. His wisdom and common sense have saved me from many 'lock-up' situations and impending disasters! Thanks too to Barney Coombes, Peter Lyne, George Tarleton, Graham Perrins, Nick Butterworth, David Matthews, Mike Pusey and John MacLauchlan, for their continuing influence on my life.

I am particularly appreciative of both the preaching and writings of A. W. Tozer, Ern Baxter, Malcolm Muggeridge, Bob Mumford, David Pawson, Robert Brinsmead, Watchman Nee and Ted Crick.

Mention must be made of the few who no longer walk with the living God but who were my friends. You influenced and enriched my life in our brief relationships. Your departure from holiness and your subsequent life-style have convinced me even further that Jesus and only Jesus is worth following, wholly and exclusively.

Then there are my many friends here in Cobham whose love and support have been beyond words. Especially the longstanding and faithful friendships of my close friend Mike Blount and colleagues Mick Ray and Martin Scott. Thanks to the various leaders of churches and fellowships up and down the country who have made platforms for me and have been glad to have me share my heart.

And finally, thanks to Anona, my best friend, faithful supporter, lover, confidante and wife. She has continued to be more than I could ever ask or expect of someone who knows me so well.

These have all had a part in my life, and therefore in this book.

Acknowledgements

Many thanks to Liz, and Jan and Hazel my secretary for their typing and re-typing of the manuscript. To Dai for checking parts of chapters and to Kingsway Publications for their patience and comments. I am also grateful to John Noble and Clifford Fryer for reading the manuscript and making several valuable and helpful suggestions. And finally to Steve who suggested I wrote the first chapter. While I have been keen to listen and learn whatever I can from these and others, I take full responsibility for everything I have written

Preface

In the history of man, there has never been such a global outpouring of God's Spirit. Renewal, reformation and revival are taking place almost everywhere it seems. Yet alongside this remarkable activity of the Holy Spirit, thousands of people in Great Britain, both young and old, are not simply disenchanted with institutional and house-church Christianity, but positively fed up with it. Especially the local variety! The lack of creativity in living, spontaneity in worship, depth in relationships and vitality in preaching, plus a new brand of 'apostolic' exclusivism, are causing a massive upheaval everywhere.

The charismatic movement is dying a death, locked up in endless singing and fashionable preaching. New wine is poured into inflexible wineskins and many are about to burst, while in some situations there are no wineskins at all—just ecclesiastical barrels! The exciting growth of the house-church movement is doomed to level off or at best grow fat and grotesque, unless something more radical— or to be precise, someone more radical—emerges. Like all men and women who seek to alter things, they will no doubt be told to quieten down and not rock the boat any further. But in many cases, despite wonderful blessings, the boat does not need rocking but positively sinking!

Because I have faith in God's ability to build his people together the way *he* wants, I have found it necessary to say what some will no doubt consider to be some hard things. But I have written with the intention of inspiring and encouraging many of you who are moving forward and looking for better things. I have also written to challenge and provoke those of you who have settled down to a lukewarm church life instead of a red-hot kingdom life. And I have, I confess, relentlessly endeavoured to disturb those of you who feel that what you represent is God's kingdom. The proliferation of your knowledge, groups, standards and lifestyle, will not of itself extend God's kingdom, bring him glory, or hasten his return, if you continue to exclude others who do things differently.

Being what one communicator called 'a vendor of words', I trust that by God's grace I shall not lose sight of the kingdom I speak of by settling for verbal statements or empires of my own! While this is not a theological book or an exposition of the Scriptures, it is nevertheless a biblically based testimony of what I believe the Holy Spirit is doing and wants to do throughout Britain. I've entitled the book *What On Earth Is This Kingdom?* not 'This *Is* the Kingdom'. For me the search as to what kingdom living means continues, and much of the road still lies ahead. But my exploration of the King and his kingdom is founded upon the historic acts of Jesus' life, death, resurrection and ascension into heaven, which the Holy Spirit has made real to me in these latter years of the twentieth century.

I have found it necessary to write a first chapter that gives a brief but I hope helpful background to the rest of the book. If the teacher teaches truth because truth is always truth, the prophet must speak truth relevant to the moral, cultural and historical setting into which he speaks.

I believe it will put the following chapters into perspective.

I have also spent a fair amount of time in the early chapters highlighting what God's kingdom *is not*. Clearing the path of accepted but unbiblical historic concepts, ecclesiastical baggage, plus our cultural captivity, is a must if we are ever to touch what this kingdom *is*! It is often needful to demolish in order to rebuild! Let's not be afraid of the bulldozer—there is an army of builders being prepared by God.

Christ, the Nazarene, Governor of this kingdom, has proved conclusively in the years that I and millions of others have known him, that he is totally just, completely reliable and utterly dependable, and is therefore worthy of being allowed to build in whatever way he wants.

GERALD COATES

The reasonable man adapts himself to the world. The unreasonable man persists in adapting the world to himself. Therefore all hope of progress rests with the unreasonable man.

George Bernard Shaw

Do not be conformed to this world [age], but be transformed by the renewing of your mind, that you may prove what the will of God is, that which is good, acceptable and perfect.

Paul (Romans 12:2)

Chapter 1

Introduction: The King, His Kingdom and Britain

It was a hot summer afternoon in 1971. David and I had walked until, tired and thirsty, we slumped down in the middle of a field. 'Well Gerald,' said David, feeling we ought to get down to business. 'What's on your heart for this conference?' I have to confess that at the time my mind was filled with pictures of long, iced, thirst-quenching drinks! I stirred myself from exhaustion. 'Well—I will tell you what I feel, David,' I sighed somewhat nonchalantly. 'I've just got this feeling that over the next few years we're going to have to ask—what on earth is this kingdom? And how does it affect our individual lives and fellowships?' They seemed weighty words for a few dozen people, at an insignificant week-long conference. Indeed they seemed wholly inappropriate. But the issue of Christ and his kingdom was one I could not get away from. Now, over ten years later, I am still the captive of this, the world's greatest theme.

What is this kingdom Jesus spent his entire public life teaching and preaching about? Why did he basically only speak about two things throughout his entire ministry—his Father and his kingdom? Why was it that after Jesus' death and resurrection Dr Luke tells us that for five or six weeks he gave himself entirely to 'speaking of the things concerning the kingdom [government] of God' (Acts 1:3)?

Is the church the kingdom of God? Is being 'born again' the same as entering the kingdom? Is it here now, or is it to come? Is it in Israel, or in the church? Can you be in the church and miss it? Once in, can you fail to inherit it? In the light of the world situation, ought we just to get on with the job of evangelizing and not worry about these theological matters? Christ, his kingdom and what it is, will I believe occupy the hearts of many over the coming years. It is to my mind the key to our history and also to our future. It is the hope for the ends of the age, and also for us as the people of God called to usher in that age.

How did we get here? (A little history!)

If what we do in our generation is unrelated to our history, then it is a recipe for disaster. 'The only thing that we learn from history is that history repeats itself,' goes the old saying.

The fifties in Britain were marked by keen evangelistic projects. Billy Graham has gone on record as saying that his return to the USA after three months' preaching in London during 1954 may have been one of his greatest mistakes. Virtually unknown in this country when he arrived, he was told by the press in no uncertain terms to go back home. However, within weeks he became headlines in the same newspapers which had earlier rejected both man and message. 'Thousands turn to Christ' the journalists wrote, and it went on unabated week after week, for months. Lesser known evangelists up and down the country became engaged in smaller but no less worthwhile efforts to bring Christ to people and the people to Christ. It was by all accounts a remarkable time. Large numbers, now in leadership among God's people, were converted to Christ during that year. Britain it seemed was on the verge of revival, but Billy went home, back to his many other commitments. Eventually the impetus was lost. It is clear that the main thrust of the fifties was evangelism.

Decade of the Spirit—the sixties

The sixties were to be altogether different. Churches were unable to absorb this new life and many converts were lost because of weak leadership, no biblical or unbiblical teaching, inflexible and outdated church structures and inexperience at coping with such a situation. It was therefore inevitable that disillusionment set in. 'There must be more to church than this,' said a growing number of bewildered but aspiring men and women. Differing conclusions as to what was needed were reached. They ranged from the call for more purity in the church and more Bible exposition to further training in evangelism.

But to a growing number the answer to the dilemma was to be found in a relationship with the Holy Spirit. If he glorifies Jesus, it was reasoned, then we need to experience more of him! To some the problems were certainly doctrinal, but it was not further doctrinal accuracy that people were longing for—important though that was—but a living and biblical experience of the Spirit. There is of course nothing like experience in Christ to change and redefine our theology! Though truth is often a gateway that leads us to the Spirit, invariably the Spirit leads us into all truth.

Michael Harper, once curate at All Souls Langham Place, stated publicly that he had been baptized in the Holy Spirit and what is more, spoke in tongues! As with anything new, the controversy was not slow to get off the ground. Had he been baptized in the Holy Spirit, or was this an overflow of the Spirit received at conversion? Were tongues for today, or was this jibberish? Did certain gifts of the Spirit disappear when the canon of Scripture was completed? Were tongues of the devil? Perhaps Michael Harper was ill or even mad!

For several years the turmoil increased. Meanwhile thousands upon thousands of people went along to Fountain Trust and Crusade for World Revival meetings, conferences and renewed churches (as they are called), finding release in the Holy Spirit. A new-found joy in devotion and praise became evident. Deliverance from demonic powers along with physical and emotional healing were frequently experienced. Jesus and the Holy Spirit were being talked about by growing numbers in virtually every denomination. Clergymen were being born again, revived with a living faith, while others were restored to Christ and filled with the Holy Spirit. Church leaders everywhere were becoming more aware of the broader issues involved in entering the Spirit-filled life.

Men in the making

David Watson, Trevor Dearing, John Noble, Don Double, Selwyn Hughes, George Tarleton, Clive Calver, Roger Forster, David Pawson, Eric Delve, Bryn Jones, David MacInnes, the late Denis Clark, Arthur Wallis, Colin Urquhart and many more were touched and changed by the breath of God's Spirit during the sixties and early seventies. Some of them were being prepared for wider ministries as a result of a new hunger for reality and a richer quality of church life. The mid- to late sixties in particular were exciting and heady days, enriched by the public statements of faith made by Cliff Richard and Malcolm Muggeridge.

As with any new move forward, there was bound to be

excess and imbalance. However, I am reminded of P. T. Forsyth who said that he would 'rather be part of a live heresy than a dead orthodoxy'. Not that it has to be one or the other! God has his own way of ironing out doctrinal and experiential wrinkles for those who are looking to live in and understand his kingdom. There were of course other important issues and conflicts going on in the church during those ten years. But to me, the issue of the Holy Spirit was of central importance. The reason was simply that God was about to bring to birth new and exciting fellowships of a completely different order from those already in existence. Such a thing could never be imagined then, but the heart and face of the church was about to change, and it would never be the same again.

Nearer to home—the seventies

While I don't believe that God works in units of ten years, it has to be said that the seventies were to become a period of God's further blessing but deeper conflict. Many began to ask, 'What is God doing and what is he doing it for?' Some endeavoured to contain their new wine in old denominational wineskins, and for several years did very well. Others felt that denominational churches hadn't a hope of accommodating the gifts and the ministries of the Spirit along with spontaneous, expressive praise, while still remaining good Anglicans, Church of Scotland, Baptists, Pentecostals, or Methodists. Others came to the conclusion that they could no longer be led by men who were either unsympathetic or even unconverted! There were others who felt unable to co-exist happily with leaders who preached against the gifts of the Spirit and resisted any significant change in church life despite the obvious deficiencies. So the exodus from institutional Christianity was underway. It was slow at first and, contrary to uninformed opinion, far from being organized, and few who were leaving the hallowed precincts of historic denominations knew what anyone else was doing in the country. So the profusion of what are called house fellowships came into being.

Our personal experience

There are still many with little accurate knowledge of house fellowships and their origins. Even if ahead of most others, our experience in Cobham was typical. We were among the first few to experience what countless others were to go through over the following twelve or thirteen years. Denominationally isolated in the Brethren and without adequate leadership, we faced conflict in our church. 'You will have to renounce this experience of tongues as being of the devil,' I was told by my Brethren elders. 'We don't believe in these things—if you don't renounce this you will have to leave.' Such a situation would be less usual today; nevertheless that attitude of suspicion and fear is still prevalent in many parts of Britain over ten years later. Our church was the only fellowship remotely evangelical in the entire town. We had no transport to commute to the preaching centres at Guildford, Woking and Walton. But renounce the Holy Spirit? Impossible! Some years earlier I had met a number of people who claimed to be Pentecostal and yet didn't belong to the classic Pentecostal churches. I wasn't interested in whether or not they spoke in tongues at the time—I had too many hyper-dispensational problems for that. What I was deeply impressed by was their enjoyment of God and life and people in particular. I had started to sing in tongues one day riding on my bicycle while singing a hymn, but I was totally inexperienced. So I contacted a Pentecostal brother whom I'd met at a conference, and he laid hands on me and gave me the final encouragement of faith. I was now committed to tongues and so out on my ear, as they say.

So my wife Anona and I began to meet with a few friends in our home. We were insecure, green as green could be, and felt that we were probably the only people in Britain who really loved the Lord Jesus but didn't actually go to church on a Sunday! We were learning the hard way that we can't *go* to church—we *are* the church!

I remember one night when we sang non-stop for almost an hour. What a blessed release from the hymn/prayer sandwich! Now Cobham is fairly exclusive by any standards, but the home we met in on that occasion was more exclusive than most.

Edwyn was educated at public school and sent off to New Zealand for further education. He returned a Christian! He tried to give his neighbours the slip the next morning as he went off to business. 'Edwyn, can you explain what was going on last night?' shouted the next-door neighbour across the drive. Edwyn's heart sank. Almost forty people were crammed in a room on a hot summer's night with the windows open, the occupants singing in tongues for almost an hour! Before he could gather himself together and defend the incident, she continued, 'We thought you had a choir in there. I got Charles to open the bedroom windows so that we could sit up in bed and listen! It was beautiful!' Due to the insecurities created by the newness of what we were doing, nobody was more surprised than Edwyn!

Going on

I remember too the real friendships we formed. Strong, honest, affectionate friendships, so different from the nice but superficial church relationships I had known. We were beginning to find fellowship based upon a shared life and not just around services and meetings. We moved house to be near each other. We began to hear comments from other residents. 'This road isn't the same as it used to be, Mabel, all these young people moving in, they're all so friendly. I don't like it!'

There was the man who stopped me in the newsagents and asked me what I did for a living. 'Well I've just left my job to help lead a group of Christians in the town,' I faltered. Then with a guffaw of laughter that brought everybody in the shop to a standstill, he bellowed, 'You've not been converted by that bloke Gerald Coates have you?' Poor man! When he found out the awful truth he went all the colours of the rainbow!

Then there were the anonymous gifts that came through our letterbox, as we lived (or nearly died) by faith. The surprise groceries on the doorstep. Backsliders from around the area turning up at our home to get right with God. Many of them moved into Cobham to join us. It has been said that it is easy leaving an institutional church to join one of the newer fellowships. Well just you try and see what happens!

We were not alone

The time came when we took our small group to London's Festival of Light, as it was aptly named by Malcolm Muggeridge. When we arrived we found almost 100,000 Christians there! Later on, Cobham was to become the centre for Jimmy and Carol Owens' musical *Come Together* organized by Jean Darnall. 'We've never turned as many as this away since the war,' the manager of Westminster Central Hall told me on the opening night of the British tour. Slowly we were becoming aware that *we were not alone*. Existing churches were waking up to the power of the Holy Spirit, and similar fellowships to our own, though small and insignificant, were springing up all over Britain in the early seventies. Some, like us, were virtually thrown out over the issue of tongues. For others it was expressive worship. For some it was daring to challenge the denominational traditions. The tension was such that people left quietly, so as not to create unnecessary conflict.

Some no doubt used what was happening to get their own way, and caused a lot of unnecessary division. They became self-appointed leaders over little groups in which they could be the boss. It is perhaps not altogether strange that some would rather be in charge of ten people than part of a body of hundreds. However, that is precisely the same as the situation in historic churches. Motives for dressing up in ecclesiastical robes surely have to be mixed, not to mention wearing a dog collar, prefixing your name with the title 'Reverend', overseeing and preaching at regular meetings—and feeling that you are someone a little special in the light of all that!

Despite the many obvious faults of the so-called house-church movement, we might as well face the fact that many of these groupings may be the only hope for God's people over the next two or three decades. God will not be tied to seventeenth-century language, eighteenth-century hymns, nineteenth-century buildings and twentieth-century religious inflexibility. I fancy that by the end of the eighties both the heart and the face of the church in Britain will have undergone such an incredible transformation that it will be unrecognizable, even by today's standards.

Moving on—together

Division, as history has taught us, is not always an unmitigated disaster. It is often a wonderful sign of life. A sign of rising stars in the face of the falling, of new light emerging as the old fades away, of new hope replacing tarnished glory. I doubt whether there is a city or town in Britain where there is not, in some form or other, a group of believers willing to forsake the 'traditions of men' and launch out with their trust in God, experimenting with new forms of unity, worship, fellowship life and commitment to God and his revealed purposes. It is in fact impossible to be committed to God unless we are committed to his purposes.

Within these groups (many of which happily co-exist alongside denominational structures and are sometimes actually built into those structures) impurities are bound to exist. As with anything new, a hint of sourness and sediment will be found, but with time, like wine, they will come to maturity. In many of these groups there has either been a reaction to institutional Christianity, or there has been a reaction on the part of the institutional Christians, almost to the point of divorce. Neither party can be expected to put reconciliation high on its list of priorities at first. But reconciliation must come, one way or another. We have much to give each other and, irrespective of groupings, Christ has given us the privilege of belonging to the same brotherhood.

A growing kingdom

Reflecting what was happening across the nation, the Dales, the Downs, Chard and Kingdom Life weeks have attracted thousands. These emphasized the importance of right relationships, friendship, commitment to one another, spiritual authority, submission, community and discipleship. Smaller weeks and weekends now abound, accommodating and underlining similar truths. On top of this British Youth for Christ's tours and concerts, the Greenbelt weekend, Wembley's Banquet, Spring Harvest and Royal Week have definitely picked up the mood of things and are experimenting with worship and different forms of platform ministry. Crusade for World Revival in large praise gatherings and seminars have for several years now emphasized the need for proper vertical and horizontal relationships. Both Youth With a Mission and Youth for Christ have also had to face the fact that after years of local evangelistic efforts in schools, universities and street theatre, converts have not been absorbed into existing church structures, and a number of centres have already become established fellowships. David Pawson is clearly stating the need for cell groups 'in every road' and the need for God's people to break out of inflexible moulds and become a prophetic people, not only by what they say but also by how they live. When God chose the nation's best known Bible teacher to be a prophetic voice—now accused of being unbiblical!—I think he must have been in a very bright and humorous mood! God seems to have taken the man regarded by most of us as safe and balanced... to unbalance us all!

So what now?

If the fifties majored on evangelism and the sixties emphasized the need for fresh power from God, the seventies found vibrant fellowships springing up outside the institutional church. These groups have in the main become fairly well equipped with a wider range of gifts and ministries of the Holy Spirit. It seems that fresh forms of community, leadership and worship are everywhere. This new life has undoubtedly revolutionized many historic churches. But wherever there have been thorough ongoing renewal and reformation, with few exceptions, there has been a clear division between those who want to move on unhindered by outdated and restrictive church practices and structures, and those who wish to move on remaining faithful to their denominational restrictions.

Of course there are those who have stayed in their denominations because they have no intention of moving on or actually doing anything about moving on, but it would be completely unfair and unjust, and more to the point untrue, to label all those in denominational churches as those who don't wish to go on with God. Then again, some groups still retain their denominational name and affiliation, even though it's disappeared off their headed notepaper and their notice board. In other cases the building has been outgrown and therefore left behind. It is a trend that will continue and no doubt there will be many who having left inflexible structures will suddenly become aware that while they were sick to death of the old order, they weren't quite prepared for the new. The transition will take time and no doubt cause a lot of heart-searching and pain.

Prophets of old?

I was enjoying supper with an octogenarian friend of mine, who relished telling me the following story.

'When I led a youth fellowship way back in 1940, Bishop Taylor-Smith was invited to speak. I remember him talking to one large group of lads telling them, "Boys, what you have done in giving your lives to Christ is the most wonderful thing you'll ever do! But I fear that in order to follow Christ fully, many of you will have to come out of existing church structures! But you are not to worry, for in that time the Holy Spirit will tell you what to do."' Deep in thought, my friend paused for a while over the meal.

He continued, 'When I saw this fresh movement meeting back in homes, just like the New Testament church, I felt this was Bishop Taylor-Smith's prophetic insight coming to pass.' Prophetic indeed. To think of people meeting in homes over forty years ago, as an alternative to meeting in institutional church structures and buildings, was outrageous. Interestingly enough, my elderly friend is now meeting and sharing life with a growing fellowship of people in his town under the leadership of his own son.

But you would be wrong to assume that the rest of this book is geared for young radicals, those meeting in homes, or those who see the house-church movement as the only viable alternative to denominational Christianity. I recognize that the vast majority of the body of Christ is still within institutional church structures in Britain. Some are extremely happy and have been helped enormously through the leadership, friendship, worship and teaching of those churches. Others are hopelessly frustrated, and it's showing! What the house-church movement are going to have to understand is that although they have pioneered in many areas, *pioneers do not pioneer on behalf of themselves,* they pioneer on behalf of others! Yes, they have explored freedom in worship, putting prophetic things into songs; yes, they have restored apostolic and prophetic ministry to the church, they are fellowships that are committed to one another and not to a system, breaking down the sacred/secular mentality, re-emphasizing grace as against law, and bringing a good measure of humour back into our shared lives together. But it is all on behalf of others.

Because this fact has been sadly forgotten, the house-church movement has already become highly sectarian in many places. It is in part positively denominational and unteachable, unless of course the teachers come from their own circle! Despite their largely unrecognized importance by denominational leaders, house-church people have completely altered our awareness of the church as the people of God. It will be seen that the house-church movement is one of the most important things that has happened to the church, and its influence is far greater than the authority it exercises. But it is not the kingdom of God! God hates monopolies and so the house-church movement in its present form will not be allowed to administrate everything and everyone under its wing, despite the obvious advantages over many archaic, unhappy and sterile denominational situations.

The swinging eighties?

If we do not learn from history, our past will also become our future. That is why I have highlighted in the following chapters what I regard to be the important issues we are going to have to face, if we are to be true kingdom people. While being biblical and therefore moral and spiritual, this book is not one of Bible exposition, or even an attempt at biblically justifying my observations and conclusions. I can only commit what I've written to the hearts and consciences of my readers, knowing that as they seek the truth and search the Scriptures, they will find direction from the Lord himself. Most groups have a tendency to swing from one extreme to another when whatever they are doing is not working. And then when the new thing doesn't work too well, they go back to what they were originally doing. However, God is not interested in what one writer has called 'pendulumitis'. God is moving in a straight line to achieve his purposes, and he's looking for a people that will follow him.

I write with the firm belief that God's people are kingdom people, that because they have come to know what he is really like, they want every area of life to come under his rule and reign. Not simply to bless them—though he will; nor even to touch the world in which we live—though we must; but rather to make God extremely happy by doing things the way he wants them done, and by doing those things the way he himself would do them.

Chapter 2

Pioneers and Settlers

'Good time away?' said one of my friends, as I returned home after three days of preaching. 'Good?' I responded, just about raising a smile. 'After being there for three days, I got some idea of what it would have been like in Pompeii, had Vesuvius been full of treacle instead of lava!' They had started off so well, but levelled off, and they were now saturated and settled to the point of immobility in their own blessing. They had worked their way through many problems, become quite free in worship, meeting in cell groups and praying for the town they lived in. But I was glad to get out of it. They had fallen in love with what they were doing and saying. They reminded me of Narcissus who, after looking at his own reflection in a pool, fell in love with himself, toppled over, fell in and drowned.

A forward-moving group is only moving forward in so far as it is made up of forward-moving individuals. A settled church, in so far as it comprises settled individuals. Jesus was no settler! In fact he was called the 'pioneer of our faith' (Hebrews 12:2 RSV). The Oxford Dictionary describes a pioneer as 'one of advance corps preparing road for troops—explorer'. My friends in Pompeii were far too settled in their blessing to move in any direction—never mind forward.

Settling for nothing

The settling church, marking time as it is, will not bring Jesus back. The second coming of Christ is not a matter of time, it is a matter of response. Response to what God is asking of the church at present. Character formation and usefulness to God and his purposes are directly related to a continual response to the Holy Spirit. A responding church will be a pioneering church. When Jesus returns, I don't want to be found as part of a company which has settled for a mixture of evangelical doctrine and charismatic worship, with a nice home, kids, fair job, a meagre measure of success, and a few prophecies thrown in. God wants us to be part of a pioneering army, beating down and cutting through the godless cultural, religious and political jungles that surround us. He wants us to be a prophetic voice and a prophetic community, declaring the heart and mind of God, not only by what we say, but also by how we live. We are to be his prophetic *now* statement to the world.

Thousands of local congregations have been lulled into a false sense of security and ease. The desire to go on and be different, to be a radical alternative, not only to the world and its systems but to the religious church systems, vanished slowly ages ago. But God in his own inimitable way is stirring the nest.

The cost of pioneering

Pioneers of course have to face the dangers, hurts, criticisms and misunderstandings settlers know little or nothing of. 'Why don't you turn that thing around?' said a friend of mine as we sat talking in my study one morning. He had been going through a particularly difficult time, criticized by friends and enemies alike, as a result of pioneering in areas of music and leadership. He was quite simply doing things differently. The 'thing' he referred to was the only framed text I had in my house at the time, positioned on my desk for all to see. 'Much is required from those to whom much is given, for their responsibility is greater' (Luke 12:48 TLB).

The temptation to settle into a quiet life is always present, particularly after a prolonged period of attack. The pioneer will have to face the fact that criticism is here to stay. Let God have his way and he will find an outlet, an expression of the life of the Spirit in you. So if you are hurt by criticism, do not give up. God will find a way to express himself through you as long as you let him have his way.

The Dead Sea is the largest hole in the earth. It is 1,286 feet below the level of the Mediterranean. It is forty-six miles long and ten miles wide in places. Around four million gallons of fresh water flow into that hole daily. But it is nine times saltier than the sea. The water evaporates under the heat of the sun and so the water level remains constant. Because of the salt density there are no fish, few plants, and very few birds as there is no food for them. The reason for all this is a simple one. The Dead Sea has no outlet! The settling church, with all of its salty resources, has at worst no outlet—and at best calculated, traditional, religiously approved outlets!

Comforting the afflicted

With a few exciting exceptions, most current preaching and teaching is largely that of comfort. 'Speak... comfortably to Jerusalem' (Is 40:2 AV) seems to be the only sort of message that most people want to hear—

particularly older people. Most hymns and choruses are full of assurance and consolation. The inference is that it is difficult to be a Christian and that it is hard to make progress, never mind pioneer. A good meeting or service is gauged by whether or not it blesses us and makes us feel good. If the speaker touches on the things we object to we react and are further entrenched in our own ideas, settling even further into inflexibility and complacency. The occasional exception occurs when the preacher gets under pressure to see the church move on, but then with a volley of frustration and sometimes condemnatory remarks, comparisons to other situations, and a good dose of hurt, all he succeeds in doing is to push believers further down their rabbit holes.

Of course the Holy Spirit does bring comfort. In fact he does more than that—he is the Comforter. The joy of his presence is often beyond words—especially in times of betrayal, failure, loneliness, or after sin has been repented.

However, many of the hymns we sing were written in times of strong persecution, and it was for such that God reserves the special ministry of comfort and consolation. Today in the West we know little or nothing of such persecution. We're comfortable, proper Christian citizens, waiting for what one radio preacher ridiculously called 'the next great event in God's calendar—the Rapture'.

It is ridiculous on two counts. First, the 'rapture preceding Christ's second coming' has been unknown to the major part of new covenant history. It has been well documented that its origins were around 1830 (see D. Macpherson, *The Incredible Cover-Up*, Logos International). One has to conclude that the secret rapture theory may be evangelical but is nevertheless unbiblical!

Secondly, the 'everything will be all right when you're dead or raptured' theology has immobilized the church. It has done great damage to a here-and-now faith, pushing

Christ's good news and triumph to some future date. There is no divine escape clause for Western Christians in the Bible. It is a grotesque idea which allows the Jews to be massacred, and Soviet Bloc believers to be imprisoned and tortured, while we 'meet him in the sky'! The rapture is a most agreeable doctrine to cowards like myself, but nothing better than wishful thinking, and must be relegated to the area of myth and fantasy.

Afflicting the comfortable

In the West the current danger for Christians does not come from oppressors who would split up our families, imprison our leaders, take away the Scriptures, martyr us, or deny us material goods. It is rather an internal disease of insulated selfishness, hardness of heart and a lack of willingness to truly love God and serve his purposes instead of our own. Many have started the course with vision and enthusiasm, only to be squeezed into the mould of the Christian/religious world. Instead of being radical pioneers, they have settled into the status quo—which is Latin for the mess we're in!

If ever we needed men and women of courage it is now. One of the reasons the church is not full of pioneers, is because it is littered with weak men who cannot control their wives, their children, or their own appetites. Sin has ruined their manhood, and in the process of restoration has almost ground to a halt. Everywhere we see frightened men—always talking about balance, the weaker brother, fear of offending people—ending up proper little diplomats. Ruled by a desire to be popular and accepted, wanting to please almost everyone at the same time, they play the peacekeeper instead of the peacemaker, and are pleasant to the point of untruthfulness.

Basically settlers are 'church' people, or, more accurately, system people, whereas pioneers are kingdom people. The clear distinctions between settlers and pioneers are set out in the table below.

I am indebted to Wes Seeliger for his original thoughts on pioneers and settlers. My own observations I've listed here.

Settlers	*Pioneers*
1. Always counting and generally resisting the cost of change.	1. 'Constant change is here to stay' is their motto. They understand that change is the essence of organic growth.
2. Giving themself to God to a degree, but it's calculated and is only 'up to a point'.	2. Daily giving themselves to God in total abandonment and utter dedication to God's known will.
3. Doubleminded, afraid of making mistakes, continually stifled, their concerns are seldom translated into actions.	3. Singleminded, unafraid of making mistakes, doers and not merely thinkers.
4. Using 'church' language— meetings, services, tradition, constitution, headquarters, balance, love (fear or sentiment in disguise), moderation, we ought to, committees, reverence, it can't be done!	4. Using kingdom language. Moving on, devotion to Jesus, obedience to his word, taking the Scriptures seriously, heartfelt worship, serving others, God's rule in all their affairs, honouring the truth, sharing what they have with others.
5. Predictable, always on time, precise over tenth-rate issues, generally middle-class, only relating to other middle-class folk, and cautious to the point of immobility.	5. Unpredictable, less concerned about time but reliable, unconcerned about class, and cautious only when it serves God's purpose.
6. Eternal life is to be safeguarded and truth defended.	6. Eternal life is to be enjoyed and explored, and truth released.
7. Concept of God—a perfect gentleman who never raises his	7. No static concept of God, having only a living

Settlers	*Pioneers*
voice, never interrupts plans already made (always agrees with and submits to the notice board), has a number of attributes some of which are better than others!	relationship. God is seen as gracious but not British, in the habit of interrupting plans made in his name that he has had little or nothing to do with.
8. The Holy Spirit is talked about in a vague, often sentimental way. He is not actually expected to do anything and is often discouraged from doing so, hence the lack of miracles, specific answered prayers, certain gifts of the Spirit, etc. He is regarded as being present at meetings and services, but in reality is only referred to when nobody knows what to do.	8. The Holy Spirit is the dynamic, active, powerful breath of God. He is God and is therefore to be worshipped and obeyed. He may be in danger of being made too much of, which is a reaction to not being made anything of among the settlers.
9. Sin is breaking with tradition, failing to observe cultural etiquette, abandoning cultural standards which are particularly offensive to middle-class, 'reverent' services/meetings. It often entails doing anything differently from the way it's been done for decades, even hundreds of years.	9. Sin is doing anything that makes God unhappy—turning back from the course God has set, failing to seek after and obey the truth. In fact a pioneer deliberately risks making mistakes so that vision, firmly implanted in people's hearts, may be implemented.

Settlers, of course, live without any warranted fear of making mistakes. They simply have no expectation other than a sad repeat of the past. For them fear dominates any forward-move; for them the only way to change is to grow into a bigger version of what they are already. Church life becomes somewhat boring, predictable and generally meaningless, but settlers don't know what to do about it. A. E. Matthews described the situation well. 'In the end I got so old and tired and weary of living, that I looked in the *Times* obituary column each morning—and if I wasn't there, I got up!' Many settlers were once pioneers, and others still have a spark of pioneering spirit left, but their faith and corporate lives are so old they are creaking, and any spark of life they have is reserved for simply helping them to carry on.

God has made it possible for us to be part of his unfolding story. Status-quo believers who love to settle may at times think they are God's gift to the earth—but personally I would have preferred a bag of fertilizer! God's most valuable gifts to the earth are those men and women who are pioneering souls. Making God's will, God's way, God's word and God's heart their utmost desire. Wishing to bring the order of heaven into the earth. Recognizing we are not merely earthly like animals, nor purely heavenly like angels, but human, straddling the animal and angelic worlds. Bringing to the earth the heart and mind, the integrity and morality of our God—and so ultimately bringing the salvation he offers.

The church is full of brilliant but settled people who could so easily play their part in God's pioneering purposes. They are, however, unwilling to make the necessary sacrifice to forge a path on behalf of others. So they must not be surprised if they are outclassed, outrun and outmanoeuvred by men and women totally absorbed by Christ and his government, men and women who go into action whatever the personal cost may be to their standard of living, denominational affiliations and personal relationships.

God is raising up a pioneering minority. It is imperfect and inadequate in many ways, but it is consumed with an utter devotion to Jesus, which though naïve at times is the only hope for the people of God. If we believe that the church really belongs to Jesus, we must let him build it the way he wants it built. Otherwise at the end of the day he may not own it. We must be willing to abandon anything which does not fit in with what is on his heart and mind. Leadership, programmes, concepts, forms and traditions that have been wonderfully blessed by God in the past, must all be laid down if God has something better in mind.

Being yourself

Pioneers will not be able to fit into existing church moulds for very long. They must be true to themselves. In the beginning God was himself with Adam and Adam was himself with God. None of us perhaps sees anything more beautiful and wonderful than God being himself with his creation, and that redeemed creation being themselves with him. Such a concept is foreign to settlers, whether they be traditional settlers or the trendy settlers whose traditions are just a little bit more modern but just as inflexible.

Authentic spirituality can be summed up in one word—reality. Settlers major on reverence—an overplayed and undervalued word. So wherever there is likely to be noise, dancing, spontaneous interruptions or a song sung more than once or twice, up goes the cry 'irreverent'. But to truly revere God is to get on and do what he wants us to do the way he wants us to do it—and that covers every area of our corporate lives together, as well as our personal devotion and morality. A lot of so-called reverence is nothing but religious superstition and sentiment that bear little relevance to God's heart or plain commands.

Reality and freedom bring us to a place where we're afraid of neither noise nor quiet. However, it is difficult praising God in silence, and there's nothing worse than calculated praise and worship! To be silent, thoughtful, restrained and subdued before the King of kings, our

Creator and Redeemer, is not necessarily reverence; it can be downright rudeness. It is hypocrisy at its worst to treat Christ as an overbearing tyrant with a nervous disposition, only worthy of our distant worship and homage, while we pay little attention to the way he's asked us to live in our relationships with all of God's people in the locality.

Religious settlers

Settlers lay great emphasis on the religious activities of the church, such as communion, elsewhere called breaking bread or the Lord's Supper. They will underline the symbolic nature of the bread and wine which for them is a reflection of their symbolic unity. How many churches are there, where even the main part of the company gathered is truly of one heart, soul and mind? Remarkably few, but settlers continue to break bread slavishly week after week as though the only thing that was wrong was the world and other denominations!

A friend of mine was in a meeting where they were about to take the bread and wine. To my friend's horror he saw a fly in the wine. With 'due reverence' the minister passed the cup around with my friend. Both were now into gross unreality. The more discerning were able to see the fly, but the cup was passed round the entire congregation. No one dared to disturb the 'holy cup'. You might be forgiven for thinking that the object of the exercise was to see if the fly was still in the wine after the sacred sip had been taken!

Such an event would be hilarious if it were not so tragic. If at the local pub the barman served a glass of beer with a fly in it, he wouldn't get away with it. No one would be likely to drink it—let alone pass it on to the person next to him.

Even as I am writing this chapter in my garden, a fly has found himself trapped in the sugary base of my coffee cup. Thus ramming home the point even further, that the thought of a refill, fly and all, borders on lunacy. Reality is not one of the dimensions that mark our times together as the people of God. The pioneer will ever be on his guard to ensure that such lunatic behaviour is not cultivated in what he's doing. It's very easy to change our liturgy and yet remain the same in our corporate lives together.

Only recently I heard of a Baptist minister who was dedicating a baby. Having prepared a wonderful talk on the name Michael, which as you may know means 'like unto God', he found himself being interrupted half-way through the service. 'Excuse me, vicar,' said the uninitiated and unconverted parent. 'His name isn't Michael, we're calling him Trevor!' The entire service was now in total disarray. 'But I haven't got a sermon on Trevor!' blurted out the minister. To me the story is so funny because I can actually see the events taking place before my very eyes with numerous ministers, house-church leaders and clergy that I know of personally!

We choose to pioneer

I believe God is currently looking for men and women who will devote their unperfected energies and personalities to pioneer in the area of making the faith more relevant to our culture. We choose to be what we are, pioneers or settlers. 'I will [I choose to] bless the Lord at all times,' said the songwriter (Ps 34:1). 'I will [I choose to] get up and go to my Father,' said the repentant son (Lk 15:18). God gives us the grace to choose. We cannot determine what this will mean or where we will end up as a result, but he does let us choose. Where the Lord guides he provides, is an old wise saying. We need not fear the future for he is our Shepherd going before us, with goodness and mercy following on behind as we refuse to settle and seek to pioneer.

The greatest men in Bible times and throughout church history were all pioneers. However, I do not believe that 'Once a pioneer—always a pioneer' is necessarily true. We may not always be at the forefront of a pioneering company, but it is vital that we are at least a part of such a grouping.

I fancy that the Pentecostal, charismatic and house-church movement may find it more difficult over the next ten years than the non-Pentecostal, non-charismatic, anti-house-church groupings. 'Much is required from those to whom much is given' is as true today as when our Lord spoke those words 2,000 years ago. We who have claimed knowledge will be held accountable to the Lord. If the newer groupings are going to settle for what they've got, within a short while they will simply be a better quality of settlers. If the traditional settlers continue to settle, despite the enormous activity of the Holy Spirit throughout the world, they will in the end find themselves resigned to faithlessness and non-expectancy of anything happening in their lives and churches.

Pioneers and settlers—a dichotomy?

It may seem at times that Scripture contradicts itself. It speaks on the one hand of Christ as a helpless, meek, available Lamb—and on the other of a kingly, strong Lion of Judah. Scripture depicts God's people as a building, a temple and in one place a city, yet in the same passage as a pure, submissive virgin bride (Rev 21:9–10).

This is so for two major reasons. First, God knows that as mortals with limited perception we cannot comprehend his nature and purposes. So he mercifully helps us with pictures, ideas, types and metaphors, enabling us to touch and grasp further understanding. Secondly, no one metaphor or illustration can adequately convey profound truth, whether it be of God or his acts of creation and redemption.

It is not unreasonable that we find Scripture exhorting us towards stability, order, peace-keeping, roots, foundations and the anchor of faith. But like every illustration, each is inadequate to describe the full breadth of God's purposes. To a shifting, disorderly rabble, disregarding authority, sober judgement and firm foundations, such exhortations would be appropriate. But to a church fixed in its methodology, inflexible in its attitudes, starchy and formal in its official dealings, the reverse challenge is a must—to move forward, break from a yoke of slavery, refusing to conform to cultural captivity. In short, to pioneer. To build even as we move forward. To make the gospel culturally relevant, to abandon archaic administrations, to live in holy obedience to God and his word. God's people must once again be gripped by this vision.

Away with the safe areas of predictability, with order which covers a mass of sin, with sentimental religiosity mouthed by generations of parrots who have no guts to do anything! Forward in humble if at times hurtful obedience to the Pioneer of our faith! On to declare by word and deed the beauty, mystery and power of Christ in the gospel! Up from a prearranged timetable, an easy-option church life, a calculated lifestyle of giving—and on to complete, continual and adoring worship of Christ our leader and King!

Chapter 3

The Kingdom of God or the Empires of Men?

Every day of our lives we are building something. It is an awesome but wonderful responsibility to know that we are building not only for the present but also for the age to come. Our proximity to Christ and to one another now is directly related to our proximity to Christ and one another in the future. The New Testament often speaks of the people of God as a building, a temple, or a city. It is obvious that the temple built during the Old Covenant and the city of Jerusalem are used as types and shadows before that 'city' appears 'which has foundations whose architect and builder is God' (Heb 11:10). John, exiled on Patmos having escaped martyrdom by being boiled in oil, not only saw a new heaven and a new earth, but also a 'holy city' (Rev 21:2). The city was made up of all the living stones who in the course of their lives were continually seeking to be shaped and fitted into whatever God was building in their generation.

All of us of course have a tendency to settle for something less than God is building—namely our own empires. Often we are motivated by fear, ambition and ignorance— and sometimes by downright evil. Our empires can be built by selfishly using our gifts, ministries, responsibilities, personalities and friendships. They will revolve around our own lives and ministries, or they may involve our families, business and church. Of course if we are in any form of government or oversight among God's people, it can be our local grouping, denomination or church work that becomes the centre of our activity. But in the final analysis God will only own what is truly his and what has been built according to his plans. He will not own our empires however hard we've worked to improve them and however much he in his grace has blessed them.

Empires need to be defended and therefore tend to be inflexible. God has designed life so that any inflexible structure will eventually have to give way to the life of his Spirit. Every knee shall bow—even stiff ones. If as individuals or groups we continually resist the Holy Spirit, simply to maintain our inflexible 'wineskins', we can expect God to judge us harshly.

The only two permanent things in life are our relationship with God and, if we are married, with our partner, although as we mature even these take on a different shape and form. They are not static. We must therefore be willing to surrender our preconceptions if they separate us from God and his ongoing, revealed purposes. Jesus is set against all forms of inflexible and institutional empire-building, whether it be corporate or private.

There are a multitude of reasons why people settle down and build their own empires, monopolizing both people and structures. God hates monopolies! And he hates religious monopolies most of all! Many monopolies and empires have been built in his name, but because they don't belong to him he does not give them direction or purpose. Their direction and purpose have been set in the heart of the builder.

There is a world of difference between *using* things for

Christ and *giving* them to Christ. There are many who will use their homes for the Lord, but would never give their homes to the Lord—he might ask them to move! There are others who will use their lives and ministries for the Lord, but will never give them into his hands. God's word often redirects and challenges, highlighting insecurities that we'd rather leave untouched. It is not that we make Jesus King by surrendering these things to him; rather we have to face the fact that he *is* King. We have to ask ourselves therefore what we are going to do in the light of that tremendous historic fact. *Jesus is Lord*—he is the King of kings, the Prime Minister of prime ministers, the Monarch of all monarchs, the benevolent Dictator of all dictators—so how does that affect me, my motivation, my ministry, the family I belong to, the redeemed community I have been joined to, all that I own and all that I want to be and do?

What are we building?

Some of us have a very limited view of building. We think of building a good character, family, relationships or perhaps success; amassing a small fortune, developing a thriving business, or simply earning a good reputation whatever the cost may be.

With these things in mind we must remember that the physical, bodily return of Christ into the affairs of men is not a fixed day set in God's diary. We can shout, preach, organize conferences and festivals, write, sing, dramatize and think about it all we like. But, as we have seen, Christ's return is directly related to what we are building and how we are building today. And, as we shall see in later chapters, it is a God-centred network of relationships that we are called to build, co-operating with Jesus as he extends his kingdom.

A change of heart and mind

Empires are built through the ingenuity, brilliance and in some cases evil intents of men. We cannot build God's kingdom. We can only co-operate. We can perceive it. And where we perceive it we must respond in the light of the fact that Christ has joined us to it. We must continually be on our guard against building our own empires. We need rather to ask God to enable us to perceive, understand and respond to what he is doing. We must never possess the work of God, for it is his possession. Rather we must serve him in what he possesses.

As we seek to be a part of God's kingdom, continually surrendering to God what we may be tempted to possess, I believe God will deal with us over certain attitudes prevalent among God's people at the moment. Let's look at four of them.

1. Jesus will not conform to our concepts

Christianity does not consist of concepts—but life! True, there are principles we are both taught and learn in the course of living. Those principles help us to understand the kingdom of God. But God is looking for kingdom *life* in which there are principles—not merely kingdom principles. The Pharisees in Jesus' day were faced with either keeping their concepts and getting rid of Jesus, or receiving Jesus and getting rid of their concepts. They decided to get rid of Jesus—and lost both!

Jesus will not conform to our concepts about what we can get out of life, how our families ought to be run, what the church ought to be like, how speakers and church leaders ought to behave, and how in fact God himself should behave towards us. When Moses faced God in the burning bush, he was recommissioned to deliver the people of Israel from Egypt. It was not surprising that he should ask for God's name. There were many gods in those days. But God didn't give him one of the many names he gave to men on other occasions to describe his nature, character and purpose. He simply said, 'I am' (Ex 3:14). In other words, when there's only one of you, you don't need a name! There is only one *living* God—the rest in fact are no gods at all.

However, an alternative rendering and one which many favour is, 'I will be what I will be.' God will not be what we want him to be. If we want perseverance or cry out for it in prayer, God may give us another dose of tribulation. The reason why is obvious. 'Tribulation brings about perseverance,' the Scripture says (Rom 5:3). Those of us who find freer forms of worship difficult want Christ to be the God of all peace and order. Those who are sick of mediocre churchianity want Christ to be radical, offensive, the upsetter of the status quo. Others of us want him to be the God of the third world, the poor and the oppressed. While others want him to be the God of the rich, the Solomons, the monarchs of biblical times who somehow were able to amass fortunes. There is a sense in which God is all of these, to different people at different times. But he will not be what *we* want him to be. He is God. And he will be what he will be. His morality, honesty and truthfulness, reliability and utter dependability, are without question. We are not here talking about a God who can't be trusted, who tells lies, who creates and destroys at will whenever the whim takes him. He is consistent—but self-determining.

We need to face the fact that God doesn't come and stand with us in what we want him to be; rather through his Son he has made it possible for us to stand with *him* in what he wants to be in any given situation. Like any Father he knows that it is often disastrous to give his children what they want, even though there are inevitably times when what they want is precisely what is good for them. But fathers determine that, not children!

So we've ended up in this nation with a religious community which claims to be Christian while maintaining a concept of God which so often is totally unbiblical. Observing this condition the population at large are continually having their concepts of God shattered. How do you square a gospel for the 'poor and oppressed' with the state church that is one of the biggest landowners in the nation? How do you square a working-class Jesus who's at home with common people, inland revenue inspectors who are bent, nymphomaniacs and prostitutes—with churches of most denominations who are continually dressing up smartly to meet one another in religious buildings? What does it do for the concepts of a naïve Bible reader who, when he eventually meets up with the so-called followers of the author of the Bible, finds that many of them don't believe in it! While we cling tenaciously to our false concepts, the world's concepts are continually shattered, and salvation disappears from view.

It is not just the world that should be having their concepts of God and his people shattered, it is the church! He will be what he will be and will not be what his people want him to be. He will not conform to their restrictive practices. It is in fact becoming increasingly difficult to keep up with what the Holy Spirit is doing among his people across the world. When I was a lad—and I'm not forty yet—things carried on much the same from one year to another, if not from one decade to another. But that's not the case now, and if we are to discover what God is wanting to do in the earth we must get to know him personally so that we appreciate what he wants to do and how he's going to do it. Like the Pharisees of old, we either receive Jesus and abandon our concepts, or defend and establish our concepts even at the risk of losing Jesus.

2. *We must abandon smallmindedness*

This is not a call to come out of a denomination. Many folk have done that and have come out to nothing. Their latter state has been worse than their former. But we must throw out the idea that God wants to extend his kingdom through folk from our own circle or group to the complete or even partial exclusion of all others. No one group has all the truth, or even a large part of it. We need each other. There must be a fresh recognition of the many gifts and ministries that Christ has put into other circles of ministry, groupings and denominations.

Jesus continually spoke out against the *system* while maintaining his love and availability for those within the system. It is current practice today, however, to criticize people from other backgrounds, running them down at every opportunity, while defending our system lock, stock and barrel—despite its obvious deficiencies. People do tend to find security in the system rather than in relationships. At least you know where you are with the system, even though it might be a case of being 'between the devil and the C of E'!

All groups tend to be built around 'it'. The 'it' is either the latest revealed thing that the group has seen, or a longstanding right that our forefathers have died for. 'It' could be a church without the Pope, baptism in water, the priesthood of all believers, the gifts of the Holy Spirit, church traditions, freedom in worship, house groups, evangelism, or the recovery of apostolic ministry. All of these are quite valid areas of restoration and rediscovery for many of us. However, once we start relating to each other on the basis of whether or not people have seen 'it' or not, we immediately build fellowship around something other than Christ and his gospel.

It is more than possible to be in a denomination and not be denominationally minded. Equally you can be in a house fellowship, giving an appearance of being non-denominational while in fact being highly sectarian. We are back to attitudes again. It is a simple fact of life that the name gives nothing away—except perhaps the point at which the revelation stopped!

3. Security must be found in God

To find security in anything or anybody other than God will eventually become a bondage. There is no lasting certainty in our safe areas. Happy are those who are still trusting God and have not got it all together. Cain received a mark from God, a sort of badge of security. But it wasn't enough for Cain. He stupidly went off and built a city in which he could make himself safe and secure, a foolish attempt at making for himself a measure of security without God.

Abraham was told to look for a city 'whose architect and builder is God' (Heb 11:10). But his descendants couldn't wait. Soon they founded their own nation, built their own city and erected a temple which eventually stood between God and his people. Anything that stands between God and his people will eventually be destroyed —even places where his praises have been sung and the Scriptures have been read, taught and expounded. God allows us to build our temples as a concession, but God has no vested interest in our man-made securities.

4. To make room for the new, we must dismantle the old

Over and over again Jeremiah was told to pull down and destroy. We all want renewal, injections of life, a little more spice added to the cake. But Christ will not build on the rubble of our past experience, and while not everything has to be demolished, there is still a lot that must be cleared before we find what is of God. The Holy Spirit has not simply come to help us do what we used to do, with a little bit more power. We cannot assume that what we have been doing for years is in apple-pie order and thoroughly pleases the Holy Spirit.

There is of course no virtue in simply pulling things down, leaving an empty building site. The dismantling we must do is to be seen in the light of the new things that God is wanting to build into our lives and fellowships. For example, I know of one church who, restricted by their hymn/prayer sandwich, abandoned any form of pro-gramme to see what would happen. Every now and then God moved among them and it was quite amazing. There was spontaneous worship, sharing of testimonies and prayer. But most of the time it was a spontaneous *nothing*! Dead as a dodo in fact. Nowhere in the Bible do we read that the church ever met together simply to see 'what would happen'. They met together with purpose—and so must we. So many of our gatherings have little or no purpose, are culturally irrelevant, and based more on the fact that something is on the notice board or church bulletin, than that the Holy Spirit is calling us together.

If we are to deal a death blow to our personal and corporate empires, these are the things that must be touched. Truth is of course unpalatable to all forms of institutional life, particularly the ecclesiastical variety. Therefore they will find these words all the more difficult. But if there is no change from the higher echelons locally and nationally, kingdom people will see through the empire-building and leave it behind. This failure to be willing to dismantle the old, making way for the new, will be seen to be the biggest single issue many of God's people will have to face.

'But things *are* changing,' denominational leaders tell me. Frankly I see very little 'official' change. The verbal pressure by radicals within denominations over democracy, bureaucracy and play-it-safe orthodoxy, will eventually prove a waste of time. Unfortunately history has shown over and over again that if you're going to do anything different, it will have to come from outside the existing inflexible empires. Today's situation could be an exception, but I doubt it.

'But the church isn't perfect,' I've heard it said. No it isn't—not least of all because it's full of people like me. But Christ wants us to dedicate our imperfect energies, personalities and gifts to his kingdom, not to our empires —neither those we build for ourselves nor those we've inherited and which we faithfully maintain at such a high cost. Every area of our lives is under the scrutiny of the Holy Spirit at the moment, and only those who are willing to be obedient will find themselves fully expressing the rule of Christ.

So I say, down with monopolies, down with empires, down with anything that has been made only by man. Long live co-operation, fellowship, and blending of our imperfect energies to move on—and not simply with the hope that we will grow bigger while remaining basically unchanged.

Chapter 4

A Kingdom Without Rules
(Law or Grace)

It was not a large meeting, but the room was packed. There was an air of expectancy as the subject was announced—law and grace. I began to speak about the lack of scriptural evidence for such things as 'quiet times', sabbath keeping, teetotalism, worshipping according to a pre-set pattern Sunday after Sunday. Suddenly a hand shot up in the congregation. 'Excuse me,' he cut in, surprising us all, 'this is nothing short of disgusting. You call yourself a preacher of the word and yet discourage the very things that the Christian life consists of. If we don't read our Bibles every morning and attend every meeting we can, where are we going to get our meat from? Every Christian should be up every morning reading his Bible and praying.'

His wife, sitting next to him, nudged him in the ribs, raised her eyebrows and loudly declared, 'Why don't you then!' Silent disorder broke out! He had been exposed, banging the drum for a cause he neither believed in nor followed. He was afraid that if his accepted standards for the Christian way of life were not preached (even if they weren't practised) his whole life would collapse. Like many others he was legalistically and aggressively defending what he felt he *ought* to believe as an evangelical.

Things ain't what they seem...

Several years ago it was in fashion for women to wear ankle-length dresses and skirts. An acquaintance of mine when preaching on one occasion implied that it would be better if the women present all wore such clothing. He had been bothered by an earlier fashion of mini-skirts that had been getting shorter and shorter as the months progressed. 'It left nothing to the imagination,' he confided, later confessing that the long dresses 'left everything to the imagination'!

The ladies in his congregation appeared to be sensitive, spiritual, modest and appropriately dressed. As it turned out it was all a cover for his own moral problems. Instead of getting the help he needed, he gently but firmly pressurized the women in his church into a pattern of behaviour which made them look spiritual and the brothers free of temptation. Nothing was further from the truth.

The church has become a mill of fantasy, grinding out the illusion that if you can't find the resources to be spiritual, you can settle for something less which looks and sounds spiritual. Many churches are run by a group of frightened men, afraid of the consequences of voicing their true feelings, and more to the point God's feelings, on a multitude of issues. They are afraid of saying or doing anything which will cause folk to leave their congregations, so that they lose their following, their pensions, their dog collars or whatever. With a number of wonderful exceptions, many of our evangelical churches preach the gospel of grace, but shot through it all is implied coercion and unstated legalistic standards of behaviour. Failure to conform to these will cause you to shoot to the top of someone's prayer list; or else you will soon be getting a visit from your cell group leader or your pastor.

We must understand that legalism with its strict view of life is at least as damaging as, if not more damaging than permissiveness, with its complete lack of truth or absolutes. It is true that a good dose of law can initially make things look better. That way life becomes orderly and problems rarely emerge—or, if they do, another dose of law will dampen things down a bit. But this is not God's answer.

Grace—plus a hand

The problem is that, although we say we believe that the grace of God is sufficient to cleanse and motivate us, we actually work very hard at making ourselves and our congregation acceptable to God. We feel we have to sacrifice, go out of our way and make continued efforts to be accepted. Sadly such activity is applauded, regardless of whether it is motivated by the grace of God, condemnation, guilt, or pseudo-righteousness. Jesus said, 'From his innermost being shall flow rivers of living water' (Jn 7:38). Not out of frenzied activity! Not out of the Bible! Not out of tradition! Not even those in leadership! Rather, out of our 'bellies', our innermost beings.

Not a few fear that if they live from their hearts they will end up in godlessness. In my opinion it is better to live as an outlaw, if that is what is in your heart, than pretend to be spiritual, where you will please neither God nor yourself. It was for precisely this reason that Jesus said prostitutes were nearer the kingdom than religious, pietistic hypocrites.

The only thing the Holy Spirit can do if we reach this stage is to convict us of our total pretence. But this is not easy, because we have kidded ourselves into believing we are pleasing God. On the other hand, if we live from the heart and find ourselves obeying the lusts of the flesh, the Holy Spirit can bring conviction as we can see ourselves moving into sin. Grace is made available to change us inwardly so that our lives become a true reflection of God's own heart.

Initially we may look a mess, but that is because we are in a mess! Jesus said, 'I am the way and the truth' (Jn 14:6). He never hid things under the carpet. Truth doesn't need a carpet. God is after genuine holiness, not pseudoholiness. If you are not truly holy, don't play-act at being holy! God is in the business of genuine love, not cultural niceness. The Holy Spirit will bring conviction with integrity, not group pressure or condemnation.

Grace means that God is doing something for me—whereas *law* means I am doing something for God. We live in a basic philosophy which is rooted in one or the other. And we must choose which it will be.

Grace to change

While God accepts us as we are, it is true to say he loves us too much to leave us that way! But God is not continually seeking to change us through pressure, coercion or placing perfectionist standards upon us.

It was Augustine who formulated the pithy saying, 'Love God and do what you like.' Augustine was not commending Christians who followed their every whim and fancy, whether it be praying or committing adultery. We are back to the heart attitude again. Either we have people doing what they basically like and enjoy because their hearts have been changed by the power of Christ, or we have them doing the right things even if they don't like doing them. That's how the church becomes filled up with people doing the opposite of what they really want. Is it any wonder that we have so minimal an effect in the world when we have people bungling their way through things they're not equipped for? Christ does not come into our lives to help us here and there, but to transform us completely, anointing our gifts and abilities, enabling us to do the things we genuinely want to do—the things he created us to do. We should not be surprised, having been correctly taught in our local church fellowship, and exposing ourselves to the influence of the Scriptures and good books, that a lot of what we want to do is in fact what God wants us to do. Simply because he has placed those desires there in the first instance! His yoke is easy, and his burden is light (Mt 11:30).

The grace to choose

Before we submit to the King and his kingdom, entering through repentance and rebirth, sin and the failure to meet our own standards are an inevitability. However, for the Christian who has submitted his life to Jesus, sin is now only a *possibility*. He has been set free to make choices that supersede fleshly desires. I often find myself praying, 'Lord, in my tiredness I choose to attend this meeting.' Or, 'I choose to be kind even though I feel I have the right to be hostile towards this person.' And often, 'I choose to be honest in this situation, when I would rather lie or bend the truth for a quiet life.' There are times when, by God's grace, we have to *choose* to give ourselves to people and not things, to work and not laziness, to communicate and not leave people guessing what is going on in our hearts and minds. Thank God for the grace to choose and co-operate with him.

While feelings are a most noble part of our life, they are not the foundation for the government of God. Righteousness lies in the will, not in the emotions. Choosing to do God's will day by day is quite often a conscious act, especially when pressures are upon us from various quarters to do other than what pleases the Holy Spirit. But we have been given grace to choose. There is no need to drift or be blown about by every stray emotional impulse.

Religious immunization

If there is no desire for God, his kingdom and rule, then surely we must conclude that such a person is not born of God. A. W. Tozer once said, 'There are many within the fold of evangelicalism who look the same as everyone else, but who have never been born again by the Spirit of God.' There is of course no procedure which will bring about a change of heart, short of a visitation from God himself. Toeing the party line and remaining religious, unaffected by the gospel and its radical implications, will only cause further immunization. Going abroad often entails injections which are in fact a watered-down dose of the real thing. Multitudes of evangelical believers receive injections regularly of that order by thinking that talking about grace is living in grace. They think they are living under grace but they've surrounded themselves with rules, laws and legislation. Standards abound, so failures abound as well! But God has something better.

Christians and rules

Does God's law apply to Christians? This is what the Bible has to say: 'The law has become our tutor to lead us to Christ, that we may be justified by faith, but now that faith has come, we are no longer under a tutor' (Gal 3:24–25). Paul is of course writing to Jewish Christians schooled in the Torah. Writing to Timothy he further explains, 'The law is not made for a righteous man but for those who are lawless' (1 Tim 1:9).

In a world that is increasingly being taken over by anarchy and those with little regard for decency, humanity and so-called Christian ethics, the only way to keep society together is to impose further legislation. So it is that we have policemen to make sure that the law is adhered to and judges to deal with the offenders. As citizens we are of course required to submit to the law of the land. If everybody failed to do this there would be chaos.

However, when we come to God's government we need to understand that he does not wish simply to impose rules, or indeed his will, on his followers. God gives us grace to change our attitudes. For example, if drivers genuinely cared for all other road users, they wouldn't drink alcohol in a way that impairs judgement and endangers lives. The increasingly, justifiably stiff penalties that are necessary would become irrelevant.

If we live according to the Spirit, continually responding to the grace of God, we don't need laws or standards. The same Spirit who caused the writers to give us the Scriptures, now lives within us and can be trusted. The tendency for people to live by the Bible without the Spirit shows more trust in the *words* of the author than in the author himself! We must understand that it is not that things must be true simply because they are in the Bible, but they are in the Bible because they are true! The truth was the truth before pen was put to paper. And the truth is that the Spirit of love, service and care for others now lives within every born-again believer.

We can trust the Spirit to lead us into all the truth. Though the truth is sometimes the door that leads us to the Spirit, always the Spirit leads us to the truth.

We should remember that it is possible to become deceived, and it is for that reason that we must give thanks to God for the Scriptures. They are an objective expression of how God wants us to live. But it is not sufficient to be merely Bible-believing—some of the most deceived people use the Bible as the basis of their position. We must be Spirit-believing and Spirit-led as well, for only a heart that continually thirsts for God, for his righteousness and truth, has the promise of being filled.

Fear of offence

'If I do just what I want and go off down to the pub, work on the garden or go down to the beach on a Sunday, am I not bound to upset people?' you ask. Yes you are! But that is where the exercise of grace becomes necessary. Unfortunately, as a general rule, I have found that grace only works one way. The man who mows his lawn on a Sunday should, it appears, cease to do so for fear of offending his brother who regards Sunday as a special day. However, few people consider the fact that maybe the brother who *doesn't* mow his lawn on a Sunday should extend grace towards the one who does! Scripture clearly states, 'One man regards one day above another, another regards every day alike' (Rom 14:5). The converted Jew, for example, may have a problem if you mow a lawn on a Saturday! If we live under the concept of not doing things *in case we offend*, we'll end up doing nothing. It's amazing how people are offended by our clothes, what we spend our money on, our homes, our children, the cinema, eating out—the list is almost endless. Often we don't know what people think of us and the way we live, generally because we're too busy telling everybody else!

At this stage it would be helpful if I drew a distinction between two types of people who become offended.

First there are those who think they know how to live and also how everybody else ought to live. They have made their standards and patterns for everybody else.

Unwritten rules and traditions caused the religious people in Jesus' day to strain out gnats from their food and drink. But Jesus told them they were swallowing camels!

These people need offending. Jesus spent a lot of time doing just that. Their gospel is bad news, hindering the life and grace of the Lord Jesus. He was not deliberately offensive; he was offensive in the course of living out the truth. For example, he healed publicly on the sabbath in the temple. He could, if he had used a bit of evangelical wisdom, have taken his sick patient behind a temple pillar for a quick pray. He could then have asked the patient not to rejoice or shout anything pentecostal, quickly slip out of the back door, miraculously healed but offending nobody. However, such 'wisdom' seemed to evade our Lord Jesus. In the full sight of watching Pharisees who were just waiting to be offended, he deliberately healed the man and so offended them all.

Secondly, our freedom does not extend to doing whatever we feel we want to do at any time. This may cause a genuinely weaker brother to fall away from Christ. Those we have already mentioned are not weaker brothers but as strong as bulls! If we know that beer-drinking, wearing denims to meetings, watching television or going to the cinema on a Sunday, will cause people to fall into temptation or sin, it is the natural thing to do to stop doing these things in front of the weaker brother. We will probably need to tell him that our action is for his sake, however, to avoid appearing hypocritical.

Since we have been married, Anona and I have had various people living with us as part of our family. On one occasion we had a young man staying with us who had been in problems with alcohol before he was converted. He had taken a sensible line of putting all drink aside. The odd glass of wine or beer was therefore out of the question. We could have had difficulties, mainly because I have never had such a problem with drink. A drink taken late in the evening or a glass of wine with a meal, and especially a mug of lager on a hot summer's day, is as natural to me as drinking tea or coffee. Jesus drank, in fact he probably drank more than I do. We were free to drink as far as our consciences were concerned, and as far as the Scriptures are concerned; but it was obvious that to do so would have been a very real cause of stumbling to this young man. So we set aside our privileges for several months and stayed off drink. Eventually he questioned why and we explained the situation.

However, as a result of living with us he came to terms with the fact that he had been cultivating a *fear* of drink, dreading even one sherry at a business meeting or social gathering. Little by little he was able to introduce himself back to moderation.

Let me quote you a cliché, as it's worth quoting: the answer to abuse is not non-use but proper use. Obviously in this case it would have been devastating if we had carried on in our freedom causing him to fall back into ungodly habits and eventually fall away from Christ. I believe such behaviour would have been gross selfishness which, far from expressing our liberty in Christ, would have revealed a bondage to our 'freedom'. Many so called radical people are actually in bondage to the law of freedom.

Love is absolute

The Scriptures are quite clear that we must not use our freedom for evil (Gal 5:13). Such things as stealing, drunkenness and adultery are absolutely wrong. Whereas kindness, purity and honesty are absolutely right. But it is not in these areas that most difficulties among Christians emerge. Our problem arises in areas where there are no absolutes, where God's grace enables us to live outside petty rules made for ourselves or others to cover our own inadequacies and insecurities.

The law-giver became the law-keeper. Now he keeps the absolutes of his royal law of love and liberty in the hearts of his people as they co-operate with him. This process of co-operating with Christ will fulfil the law of God in our lives. It is nothing short of a twentieth-century miracle. Sadly many believers have a completely wrong idea of the law and of God's absolutes.

Punch magazine once carried a cartoon of Moses descending the mount with two large tablets of stone underneath his arms. Below were the people waiting to hear what he had to say. Underneath was the caption, 'Well fellahs, this is only the first draft, but it seems nobody is going to get away with anything!' It is not, however, God's intention to demand a moral excellence which he knows his people will find totally unobtainable. He has given us all things that will cause us to be like himself. He does not want a sin-centred and sin-oriented people, but a people that is Christ-centred and Christ-oriented. The evangelical gospel that majors on the cross misses the whole point of the gospel. The cross alone is not central to salvation—it is Christ's death and resurrection that are central. If there were no resurrection, no risen, glorified Saviour and King, the cross would mean nothing. It is the fact that there is a glorified man in heaven, who was crucified for our sins and is now living his life in and through us, that is so absolutely fantastic. To say it's good news is a major understatement! The Christian life is not a cross-centred, sin-centred faith, but a cross-and-resurrection-centred faith. A holy, joyful, victorious faith, setting us free from false standards and concepts and all forms of legalism.

Sadness and disappointments there may be, but even

they will be shot through with the grace of God and reality.

Chapter 5

Pilgrim's Progress

According to my observation, the modern Pilgrim's Progress follows a fairly routine pattern. On hearing the gospel the hearer is often overwhelmed with a sense of sin and separation from God. After receiving forgiveness, he is helped and counselled by those who know and love the Lord Jesus. Then 'Lawson' (what more appropriate name?) is quietly but firmly encouraged to join a gospel-honouring congregation, pray regularly (every day), read the Scriptures daily without fail, and take responsibility in the local church. Several months go by and eventually he returns to his counsellor, admitting defeat and failure in many areas. 'Lawson, who do you think you are—you cannot hope to keep the whole law. That is why Jesus died to save you and forgive you. You'll be a sinner till the day you die!'

Launched on a problematic course by being told he'll be a sinner till the day he dies, while striving for perfection, his fate is sealed. It is as possible to build a stable Christian character on such uncertain doctrine, as it is to build the Post Office Tower on foundation bricks of ice cream!

Confused by being told that he would be a sinner till the day he died, and subject to continual strong inferences that he ought to be sinless, doing all the right things, believing all the correct doctrines, the pressure is now on to fit into the religious system.

A false start

Next Lawson has to merit membership in his local church. Confirmation is necessary (maybe by a bishop who is not remotely evangelical or even Bible-believing) or maybe water baptism—but not just yet of course. After all he may not understand what baptism is all about. (Not that one gets the impression that converts 2,000 years ago knew all that much about it either.) After some months of learning and conforming, he is allowed baptism or confirmation and, almost as a reward for good conduct, welcomed into fellowship.

A dangerous principle is forced upon Lawson from the start of his church life. Namely, prove yourself, do well, fit into the pattern of things, and God will bless you—and more to the point so will your brothers.

Found to be trying

Lawson has a go at 'quiet times' but oversleeps. Frequently! He feels a failure. He goes out witnessing regularly in the church team, often ending up either aggressive and rude or religious and unreal. But still he has the highlight of the week to come—communion, or the Lord's supper. Sunday after Sunday as a mental gymnast he indulges in nothing short of mental idolatry—conjuring up in the stillness a mental image of the middle cross and a darkening sky behind, with the mob on the side of the hill. No one ever tells him that he may express with joy Jesus' death and its triumph and accomplishment. He struggles beneath the law of having to feel something religious at a particular hour on the first day of the week. He tries to be thankful. Occasionally he succeeds, producing the rosy warmth of pride, but normally he sinks into further condemnation because the emotional response hasn't happened.

It is not so much that these things are wrong in themselves, though some of them may be. Rather, it is the spirit in which they are done. An enforced legalism all in the name of grace. A gospel which says it's Jesus and nothing else that saves us—but a life-style that declares something quite different. I challenge the validity of a communion service taken with loads of people who probably are not born of God. I challenge a breaking of bread service slavishly practised by people who don't get on with one another. The whole thing of course is a farce; it's a sort of bad joke, a grotesque caricature of something which should have been full of life and meaning.

Give it a rest!

Consider the question of a disappointed and bewildered Paul to the Colossian church: 'If you have died with Christ to the elementary principles of the world, why, as if you were living in the world, do you submit yourself to decrees, such as, "Do not handle, do not taste, do not touch!"' (Col 2:20–21). The Colossians equated Christianity, quite falsely, with reformed Judaism. The modern emphasis upon the recognition of Sundays, a complicated calendar of holy days, religious buildings, clergy/laity, is all a hang-over from the Old Covenant and is crippling the simplicity of pure gospel liberty.

Many of the early Christians do appear to have escaped this Galatians/Colossians half-breed religion. We learn this from the writings of one of the church fathers, Justin, in the account of his dialogues with Trypho, a critic of the believers' way of life. In his first charge against Christians, Trypho refers to their wicked abuse of the sabbath. 'This is what we are most at a loss about. That you, professing to be pious, and supposing yourselves better than others, are not in any particular way separated from them, do not alter your mode of living from the natives, in that you observe no festivals or sabbaths, and do not have the right of circumcision. And further, resting your hopes on a man who was crucified, you yet expect to obtain some good things from God while you do not obey his commandments.... Have you read that the soul shall be cut off from his people who shall not have been circumcised on the eighth day?'

In fact the early church believers normally worked on Sundays with the rest of the labouring world, until Emperor Constantine set Sunday apart as the official holy day in A.D. 321. God bound Israel to his law at Sinai. But he never imposed a special national day on Gentile people. One day in seven was all God expected of Israel, but in Christ he has provided not merely one day of bodily rest, but eternal peace with himself and the brotherhood and, as much as is possible, with all men everywhere.

Jesus and the law

It is of course true that Jesus carefully kept all the ceremonial requirements of Moses' law; circumcision, Passover, and the rest. Yet we must understand that he observed these regulations during his life, simply because the New Covenant did not come into force with his birth, but with his death and resurrection. He died for the lawless in order to grant forgiveness to repentant lawbreakers. He then rose and ascended into heaven, filling pardoned outlaws with his Spirit. Christ not only kept the law but is now keeping it in all of those who have been washed in his blood and received his forgiveness. 'For to me, to live is Christ,' shouted Paul (Phil 1:21).

Salvation thrives on life, not laws, and salvation begins with reconciliation—not regulation. The early church were together *every* day, worshipping and praising God. Not simply on Sundays. They didn't *go* to church, they *were* the church!

That the human body needs rest and that one day of rest in seven is a good principle is not in question. But there is no divine statute to specify which of the seven. Too many devoted churchgoers are physically and mentally over-worked on Sundays! Very few congregations in fact spend much time in restful worship on the first day of the week anyway. They abound in preaching, teaching, testimonies, studies, Sunday Schools, open-airs and discussions. Heartfelt worship expressed in songs or quiet contemplation would barely clock up more than a total of half an hour. And much of that would barely rate as real worship, even by Old Testament standards, where songs were accompanied by musical instruments, dance punctuated with hand-clapping and shouts of joy—interspersed with prostrations and awe-filled silences. God is sovereign and often blesses us in our legalistic routine, whether it be ASB, the hymn/prayer sandwich, or endless choruses. But let us not draw the false conclusion that our restrictive or legalistic expressions of worship merit his blessings.

Grace and law will never settle for peaceful co-existence. One must be evicted. When the believer properly fulfils the royal law of love, for God and his neighbour, he renders the law obsolete. This is a kingdom of unending grace, not unending legislation. If the devil cannot prevent the sinner's conversion, he will intimidate and bind him in a prison of introspection and failure. There is of course a place for healthy self-examination, but not introspection. That is like peeling layer after layer off an onion—

eventually you get down to nothing.

It is more than possible to end up slavishly adhering to traditions, breaking God's 'law of liberty' and love (Jas 1:25). It is less likely that we shall keep that law and break with inflexible, Spirit-quenching traditions. But that is precisely what we are called to do. The law is now written on our hearts (Jer 31:33) so that law-keeping becomes an activity of the Spirit, born out of our love for Jesus the supreme Law-keeper. Thus there is no need for constant reference to an external set of rules, God-given or otherwise.

The pilgrim and culture

The first Spirit-filled community of pilgrims were mainly Jews. They were eager to show others that Jesus had made them 'complete'. They enjoyed a good reputation and worshipped in the temple, circumcised their babies and did all the things that faithful Jews should do. Paul even had his friend Timothy, a grown man, circumcised so that he would not be regarded as having gone off the rails. Peter, several years after his conversion, stated emphatically that he had 'never eaten anything unholy and unclean' (Acts 10:14). We also read that Paul honoured Ananias for observing the law (Acts 22:12) for which he gained the respect of the Jews. Yet the same Paul, whose main ministry was to the Gentiles, realized that once he had left Jerusalem and the Jewish believers, the gospel and the morality of Christ had to be interpreted into a different cultural context.

Within a few short decades, the non-Jewish saints outnumbered Jewish believers. Jerusalem was eventually overrun by her violent enemies and the church and its leaders escaped for their lives. It was at that time Jerusalem lost its control on what had become known as Christianity.

Yet even before this there were plenty of radical fellowships where there were both Jews and Gentiles relating together. In the light of this new situation they had to ask themselves several important questions. What does one eat and not eat when offering hospitality? It was agreed that non-Jewish believers should be asked to abstain from eating meat offered to idols, strangled animals or blood. They were of course forbidden to indulge in any form of sexual immorality, but were asked to make no other considerations (Acts 15:28–29).

The church also had to come to terms with the fact that in the Roman world Saturday was not a public holiday and Sunday was not a holiday for servants and slaves. And so the church was about to burst out of its cultural and historical limitations. It was no longer to be restricted by Jewish forms, traditions and history.

The Jewish pilgrim and the law

In the Pharisees' minds there were 630 or more commandments that were all looked upon as God's word and therefore to be obeyed. The breaking of one law was the breaking of it all. They could not be selective in what they kept. 'Cursed is everyone who does not abide by all things written in the book of the Law, to perform them' (Gal 3:10). It is all or nothing. If one part is broken, all is broken. If you don't circumcise your children, you've broken the law. If you don't keep the sabbath from Friday evening to Saturday, you've broken the law. If you take your car to church, you've broken a 'sabbath day's journey'. You can't bend the rules. You either keep the law or abolish it. You can't have it both ways.

Why the law then? The law was a temporary measure until Jesus came (Gal 3:19–25). The Jews were governed and disciplined as children by all sorts of rules and regulations. Those who still major on striving to keep the law—moral or ceremonial—fail to understand that such behaviour is not maturity but gross immaturity.

Paul, as we know, was a great lover both of the law and his Jewish culture and tradition. He had this remarkable devotion which caused him to harass born-again believers, divide families and initiate and oversee a murder. But such was the radical transformation that hit him on the Damascus Road, that he later withstood his friend and colleague Peter, also a Jew, over the issues of law, culture and tradition (Gal 2:11–14).

Peter was not doing anything contrary to what had been expected of Jews for centuries, yet Paul rebuked him in no uncertain terms because he was 'not straightforward about the truth of the gospel' (Gal 2:14). This situation proves conclusively that it's more than possible to obey what is written and still do evil. A rule book cannot produce godly character. Rule-book churchianity will never satisfy God's heart.

Pilgrims progressing...

Paul of course understood why God gave the Jewish people complicated rules, magnificently dressed leadership, holy buildings and strict legislation about food and drink. It was simply because Christ had not come. They were, as Paul clearly stated, 'weak and miserable principles' (Gal 4:9 NIV), shadows of a better covenant to come.

Writing in desperation to the believers across Galatia who had failed as a pilgrim people to come out of the Old Covenant into the New, he wrote: 'For in Christ Jesus neither circumcision nor uncircumcision has any value; the only thing that counts is faith, expressing itself through love' (Gal 5:6 NIV). The impact of those words cannot be understood by those of us who are not Jews. What he is saying, quite simply, is this. In terms of God's government, or his kingdom, what you eat, how you spend your time, whether you drink alcohol or not, circumcision, sabbath-keeping, quiet times, are all irrelevant apart from faith in God and love for one another, which is the essence of what God requires. 'Carry each other's burdens, and in this way you will fulfil the law of Christ' (Gal 6:2 NIV). God did not intend non-Jewish believers to have such things as sabbath-keeping, food laws and sacrificial laws imposed upon them. The law was now written on their hearts, it is true, but that law had to do with a sensitivity to their responsibilities to God and neighbour.

It is no good taking bits of the Jewish culture and trying to make them into Christian culture. There is no such thing as Christian culture along with a few Christian laws. Jesus came to give us life—life which is higher than law, life which invades every culture.

Pilgrim morality

The Jews fought for the law and their culture because they claimed it was given at Sinai—at the birth of their nation. But Paul argues that his gospel goes back even earlier than that! It was announced to Abraham 400 years before the law was given (Gal 3:8–17). While the curtain was down for the majority of people, Abraham lifted a corner, as it were, and glimpsed the age that was to come.

God's purpose required that the Jewish nation keep their distinctive identity until their Messiah, the Saviour of the world, stepped into history. In order to do that, they had to be a people living apart from all other religions and nations. God therefore declared that certain foods were unclean. However, Paul later states that 'no food is unclean in itself' (Rom 14:14 NIV). The establishing of rules, laws and bye-laws had the practical effect of keeping the Jewish nation separate from all other nations and religions. Their gods would only accept sacrifices at special places. Religious places are generally associated with religious mountains. So Mount Zion was set apart as a place for the people of the living God to come and worship. God separated them geographically from other religions. Yet when the woman at the well asked Jesus whether it was the hilltop denomination or the establishment denomination which was acceptable to God, he told her that she'd missed the whole point of worship. In the final analysis it is not the geography but the heart that counts.

Jesus commissioned his disciples to go to Jerusalem, where their friends were; to Samaria, where their enemies were; and to the uttermost parts of the earth to proclaim the gospel which was to cut through every cultural barrier.

The new Jewish people, Hebrew Christians, born again as they were, were not now to be kept separate, but to infiltrate the world taking the message of reconciliation and salvation wherever they went.

This gospel declared that the repentant criminal should be received and accepted solely on the grounds of the wonderful fact that Jesus is the substitute for the unrighteous, taking the full impact of the penalty for sin. A man is spiritual only because of his relationship with Christ. In fact Paul preached so much grace he eventually had to answer the question 'Are we to continue in sin that grace may abound?' (Rom 6:1 RSV). It was of course a logical conclusion, that if things are this good and it's better after you've sinned than before—let's go ahead and have a jolly good sin-up! J. B. Phillips translates Paul's stoccata reply: 'What a ghastly thought!' (Rom 6:2).

The twentieth-century scandal

It is therefore scandalous as well as unbiblical for the modern-day people of God to fill what corporate lifestyle they have with bits and pieces of Judaism, altars, special priesthood in ridiculous outfits, and an updated version of the elaborate Jewish calendar—plus all the other minor, but no less crippling legislation we have in churches today. In this we have made a false divide between believer and unbeliever, saint and sinner. It is vital that the differences be seen in terms of our morality and righteousness, rather than our cultural lifestyle.

The law is vital in so far as it maintains a restraining influence on society. It also points out disobedience, selfishness and sin, and draws in the offender to look to Christ for forgiveness and reconciliation. But 'the Law made nothing perfect' (Heb 7:19), even if it was perfectly kept!

Forward!

An inch in the right direction is better than a mile in the wrong one. The road to recovery is bound to be slow, but the Holy Spirit is moving at a remarkable pace today. For many of those bound in legalism and tradition, it will become increasingly difficult to catch up with what the Spirit is doing. The charismatic movement and the house-church administration could well be a fairly healthy limb on a very sick body. But I fancy as time progresses, and the church in Britain is absorbed more fully into the culture of the nation, that the gap between newer expressions of corporate life and traditional will widen enormously. Our corporate gatherings and individual lifestyles must reflect the culture in which we live, and in historic denominations nothing could be further from the truth. The gospel of the kingdom calls into question all we believe and all we do—corporately, as well as in our individual lives. That gospel determines our view of everything else, and, as I have already said, that gospel frees us from much of what passes for normal church life.

Malcolm Muggeridge has said over and over again that he believes that this is the end of Christendom as we know it, and I fancy he's right, even if he has briefly joined it! The false security systems of Sundays, saying 'grace' at mealtimes, abstinence from certain foods and drinks, and so forth, can only cushion us from the ultimate crumble of Christendom. The world is not impressed. Such systems merely delay the time when we have to face the real issues. God is bearing in on his pilgrim people, overturning the idols we cherish so much, things he has even apparently blessed at times, although he is now in the process of sweeping them away. For he *will* sweep away all that we trust in other than himself. In my opinion such turning points only come every few decades—but we are at one now! It's no good building systems for ourselves, however historic, fanciful or modern. They will not protect us from the unknown future. We have to be done with the lie that God builds systems. God is calling us to beat the system. Not only the world system but the religious system too.

Slave or free?

All systems eventually become oppressive slave-structures, grinding people down until they find themselves so secure in their bondage that, like battery hens, they don't actually want to be freed at all. Systems—patterns of doing things— whether they be individual or corporate, set Christian against Christian and prevent any intimate fellowship.

The old ways may have been helpful, in fact at times have been the only thing around. But we have to confess they cultivate restrictive and at times inhibiting practices, whereas God is doing a new thing. Just because something was right for Luther, Calvin, Wesley, the Jeffries Brothers, or J. N. Darby—it doesn't mean it's right for us.

As pilgrims we have no lasting city here, and many to whom we have looked in former years are now either dead, or if living, out of touch with the new thing God is doing. We must move on. We live in a fantasy world if we think that God's purposes in Britain will be furthered by singing the old hymns with the same old faces, following the same old pattern of services, teaching the same old emphases, and standing for the same old causes.

Long live freedom! The kingdom of God liberates us to truly love God and serve those around us. Of course it will entail gathering with God's people, reading the Scriptures and talking things out with Father, but that will be because of a basic desire to do so—not simply because we *ought* to! The gospel liberates wherever it goes, facing people with the true value of life, love, freewill and the potential of a relationship with the living God, Creator and Redeemer of the earth! He is changeless yet he is moving on, calling us to further exploits, challenging us to be a pilgrim people.

Therefore... 'Let us also lay aside every weight and sin which clings so closely, and let us run with perseverance the race that is set before us, looking to Jesus the *pioneer* and perfecter of our faith' (Heb 12:1–2 RSV, italics mine).

Chapter 6

A Kingdom Free from Sin

Mike shared his problem with me, falteringly but sincerely. 'Since you gave me that paper you wrote on sin and forgiveness, I've been in serious difficulties,' he began. My heart sank. I had been preparing for a small publication entitled *Free from Sin*. 'Oh, how's that?' I said with some hesitancy. 'Well,' he continued, 'before I read your article, I used to go to bed every night, and go back in my mind over the day, confessing to the Lord all the sins I could remember. However, since I read your paper, when I go to bed I can't even think of anything to confess! I really can't. I go from day to day sometimes without any conscious awareness that I've deliberately or knowingly sinned against God!'

I breathed a sigh of relief. 'Well, that's fantastic!' I responded.

'Fantastic?' said Mike. 'It's terrible! How can you live for a whole day without sin? It can only be pride. What shall I do?'

An obsession with confession

So convinced are we that as Christians we are sinners by

nature, that the man who keeps confessing his sins is looked upon as being more holy than the man who in the main is free from sin. Sin and repentance have become spiritual, while holiness is still suspect! John Wesley had the same problem. While preaching on the theme of 'Christian perfection', he had this to say:

> There is scarce any expression in holy writ which has given more offence than this. The word perfect is what many cannot bear. The very sound of it is an abomination to them. And whoever preaches perfection (as the phrase is), that is, asserts that it is obtainable in this life, runs great hazard of being accounted by them worse than a heathen man or the publican.

One thing we need to be clear about: *it is not spiritual to sin*. The majority within the fold of evangelicalism would agree that scripturally the practice of sin is abnormal. That holiness of life is the norm for the Christian. However, most well-meaning Christians are obsessed with confession. It also has to be said that many others are so insensitive to the Holy Spirit that an occasional official apology to the Lord is the most that can be expected!

God has given us a life which cannot sin (1 John 3:6). However, we may not always live from the source of that life. We sometimes live according to the inclinations and passions of the flesh. But we must understand that the basis of our Christian life is *not* that we are sinners coming into sonship. We are sons of God right now, and we're being changed daily from one degree of glory to another as we co-operate with the Holy Spirit.

If we are going to honour God and be free from habitual sin, we must know our enemy.

Be prepared!

In the area of military conflict, attacks come from air, land and sea. Therefore the Ministry of Defence employs its forces in three categories for counter-attack. Namely the Army, Navy and Airforce. A formation of supersonic jets would hardly manage to chase a group of saboteurs down a back alley! An armoured-car division would not really do the job of fighting enemy warships at sea! The defence system must match the particular type of enemy activity, and this holds true in spiritual warfare as well.

Satan can attempt to draw us out from living by the Holy Spirit only by variations of his three categories of temptations. These are the flesh, the world system, and his army of demons.

1. The flesh

We must distinguish very clearly between the flesh, as referred to in the New Testament epistles, and the human body. The body is not evil but wonderfully designed by the Creator. The devil did not invent physical pleasure—that was God's design. The enjoyment of food to the palate, music to the ear, beauty to the eye, fragrance to the nostrils and feeling to the touch, was all in God's heart and mind when he created man.

The believer comes under the dominion of sin when he acts in independence from God, allowing his appetites to rule. The flesh knows nothing of the lordship of Christ. It wants to dictate moves, decisions and plans. But God intends that his children should enjoy his rule and not suffer the dictatorship of the flesh. This is kingdom living. The flesh will never improve and its sins cannot be refined. Once we are born of the Spirit our souls (i.e. the intellect, emotions and will) are being saved day by day, and our bodies await the ultimate redemption, when immortality will swallow up all fleshly inclination. 'Therefore we do not lose heart, but though our outer man is decaying, yet our inner man is being renewed day by day' (2 Cor 4:16).

God never intended civil war between spirit and flesh. Once a person has by God's grace chosen to do his will, an amazing transformation of attitudes, morals and affection takes place. The life that God has given us does not get arrogant, untruthful, resentful or temperamental (90% temper, 10% mental!).

Paul writing to some Italian believers at Rome said concerning the flesh, 'Consider yourselves to be dead to sin, but alive to God in Christ Jesus' (Rom 6:11). At conversion, God gives us a fresh spiritual appetite, but if all we feed ourselves on are novels, radio and television programmes, cinema films and superficial conversations, it is hardly surprising we are going to have difficulties walking in the Spirit and resisting the inclinations of our flesh. It is not that these things are wrong in themselves, but they are an unbalanced diet. The reason many people do not grow spiritually lies in what they feed themselves on. We need to train our faculties to appreciate the beauty of God's creation, read and absorb the Scripture, as well as submit ourselves to teaching (public and private) from friends and leaders.

We have already seen that sin is no longer inevitable when we become Christians. We must not live continually struggling with sin, but rather put all that behind us. If we maintain a proper diet, we shall find the Holy Spirit committed to transforming us. It is not our job, it is his—we simply have to co-operate. Eventually we will be presented to God 'without spot or wrinkle' (Eph 5:27)— without the spots of immaturity and adolescence, or the wrinkles of old age and senility. We'll be presented mature. We must stop *trying* to be perfect, dedicating our imperfect energies to doing God's will. Righteous choices lead to healthy emotions and a strong spirit. As Donald Grey-Barnhouse once said, 'You see to it that you do right, and God will see to it that you come out right.'

Sex and the flesh

Whenever the flesh is mentioned, sex normally looms large in most people's minds—especially young people's. For biological reasons this is perhaps more true for men than women. I believe this basically stems from picking up most knowledge about sex from the world system. Our attitudes and values come from the media, friends at school and university, and out of an almost total lack of education and teaching by Christian leaders. It is not therefore unusual for young men in particular to be bothered by continual masturbation until they are married, and it doesn't always stop then.

God wants us to celebrate our manhood or womanhood and not be afraid of it. He wants us to give thanks for our normal sexual impulses and emotional responses and not push them down fearing what will happen.

Over this whole issue of masturbation we have to face the fact that the Bible is completely silent about it. The men who lived 2,000 years ago had all the same basic desires and inclinations of twentieth-century man. In the light of the fact that the New Testament continually encourages us not to get drunk, rob, murder and swindle, it is amazing that the one thing that most Christian men actually do isn't even mentioned!

Compulsive masturbation simply for the purpose of self-gratification, and with other people in mind, is sin. It reduces those we think of to sexual objects, and cultivating such mental fancy does positive damage to friendships and fellowship. But masturbation for the purpose of self-control is something altogether different. The act of masturbation in itself is not a sin. When someone is under pressure to the point of continual distraction, it is often best that they take steps to relieve themselves. No mental stimulation is necessary—no magazines to gloat over, no driving compulsion!

I know of many leaders who have given wonderful counsel to people who have been 'delivered' from masturbation, but on further enquiry I find that they have rarely gone back to the people they've prayed for to find out if there's really been any change! I've no doubt that there are many people who are wrongly given to habits and who do need prayers for deliverance. Permissiveness precedes possession. However the issue is not masturbation, but the question whether we are *bound* to do it. We should treat that on the same level as bondage to other normal appetites such as drink, eating, leisure time, Bible study, music (classical or rock), money, and so on. Many of these things are neutral in the kingdom of God; it is our attachment and bondage to them that makes them sin. We are not to have anything or anybody rule over us, except Christ himself.

Sinners by nature? No!

All temptation comes from outside of man. It's not surprising to find colours, shapes and textures stirring up passions, feelings and our mental and academic faculties. It is not an evil thought that is sin, but evil thinking. Not an angry feeling, but sustained anger leading to resentment and bitterness. 'Sin is crouching at the door' (Gen 4:7). And all around us is proof that the things I've already mentioned can be used for legitimate or illegitimate purposes, depending on our reaction and morality.

It is no longer in the nature of the born-again, Spirit-filled believer, to be continually doing things which cause Jesus pain. It is no longer within the warp and woof of the believer continually to sin against God, the brotherhood and those around him. Our desire is now to do the things that please the Lord. There will be failures, shortcomings, and at times even outright disobedience. But an acknowledgement of our foolishness, stupidity, ignorance or wilful attitude, and an apology to the Lord plus a desire to do better next time, will bring about God's forgiveness and cleansing. 'If we confess our sins, he is faithful and righteous to forgive us our sins, and to cleanse us from all unrighteousness' (1 Jn 1:9).

2. *The world*

God wants us to be in the world but not a part of it. Many Christians are very much a part of the world but not in it! Most are too busy running round from meeting to meeting, voluntarily or involuntarily, to be very involved with the world. Work is looked upon as a necessity, the family a privilege, and the rest of life is made up of meetings of one sort or another. The values of the average Christian are not very much different from his unconverted next-door neighbour. It's just that he has other things—albeit important ones—tacked on.

What is worldliness? It is not what many Christians believe it to be. True spirituality cannot be assessed by our standard of living, what we eat and drink, how we spend our money, and how much we enjoy a particular part of our culture. Worldliness, quite simply, is an attitude of heart.

The Christian who never opens his home to the new convert, or indeed the unconverted, in case they spoil it—has a worldly heart. We become or remain worldly by adopting the standards and values that society in general puts on things. It has a lot to do with money and our attachment to *things*. Paul said, 'The love of money is the root of all evil' (1 Tim 6:10 RSV). The world is a very beautiful place, despite its terrible injustices, obvious trouble spots, depressed areas and tragedies. However, Jesus was not enduring his thirty-three years in the world, he was enjoying them! It was his world; it belonged to him. He created it and one day will redeem it back to himself, when there will be a new order of heaven and earth.

Retreating from the world, its noises, colours, shapes and culture, into a cloistered and religious atmosphere is not what Jesus has in mind. However, we do need to face up to the fact that the world can pull us away from our relationship with God. If we are to live in the world and enjoy its benefits, despite its fallenness, there is always the strong temptation to adopt its standards and ideals as well as its false values.

Religious and selfish

Mark was certainly not wealthy, but by any standards he was fairly comfortable. His wife and children were well looked after, their home nicely furnished, clean and tidy. The car, though a recent model, was looked after like a veteran by a car fanatic. As far as his business was concerned, it had to be said he was a hard worker, reliable, dependable and always ready to give that extra bit more. He was devoted to his wife and children, with whom he spent most of his time—apart from times spent on the house and garden and attending Christian meetings. He was no bother to his Christian community, whether in terms of his behaviour or failure to fulfil his responsibilities. He attended all the meetings, helped folk out especially in times of crisis, and probably by church standards gave above average financially into the central offering.

Yet shot through this young man's life was an attitude so identical to his unconverted neighbours, you could hardly tell the difference. True, he went to church and had many Christian friends. Occasionally he was over-whelmed with thankfulness to God for the good things of life. Yet he was running his entire life, home and family *for* the Lord, without ever *giving* it *to* the Lord. He never questioned whether the Lord wanted things that way. His models for life were based on what he could see from the best worldly families, the only difference being that he frequently thanked God for what he had.

'Can I borrow your car?' somebody asked him one day. He nearly keeled over. The thought of loaning his car to anybody was the furthest thing from his mind. He made the supreme sacrifice. 'I'll drive you wherever you want to go,' he said, feeling he had at last achieved something in this area. 'Well actually,' the carless person continued, 'I was wondering if I could borrow it to go on holiday!'

Mark looked astonished, so the request was pursued even further. 'You don't seem to use it for work, in fact it's only used at weekends.' I won't go into the long story that followed, but suffice it to say that he never did loan the car even though it didn't leave the garage all week!

On another occasion, it was brought to the attention of the group of believers Mark belonged to, that another brother was in need over the purchase of a small house. They had decided that this was something they wanted to support, and they arranged to take up an offering. The house was smaller than the one Mark lived in, had no central heating, and no carpets or furniture in it. The brother in question simply wanted to purchase the property, starting from the bottom and working his way through, making the best of what he had. When Mark heard about it he was in immediate problems. 'I didn't have an offering when I got married,' he bleated. 'If he couldn't afford to live in the house, he should not have started negotiations.' So, despite money in the bank to pay his bills, cash for holidays, a car and fairly complete home, not to mention a sufficient supply of clothes, five pounds was all he put in the offering. And I fancy that was to save face!

Fancy a squeeze?

Man becomes what he morally glories in. 'Don't let the world around you squeeze you into its own mould, but let God remould your minds from within, so that you may prove in practice that the plan of God for you is good, meets all his demands, and moves towards the goal of true maturity' (Rom 12:2 in J. B. Phillips' translation).

Our minds need to submit at all times to the mind of Christ. We should set our mental sights in a vertical position and not on the horizontal. Being heavenly-minded makes us of great earthly use! 'Whatever is true, whatever is worthy of reverence and is honourable and seemly, whatever is just, whatever is pure, whatever is lovely and lovable, whatever is kind and winsome and gracious, if there is any virtue and excellence, if there is anything worthy of praise, *think* on these things, fix your *minds* on them' (Phil 4:8, italics mine).

The world system—its media, goals and values—tells us that the good life, the satisfying life, is found in *things*. Jesus came with a liberating message: 'Man shall not live on bread alone' (Mt 4:4).

The advertising world declares that a splash of this, a drink of that, a drive in this and a set of clothes made of that, hair looking like this and bodies like that, freedom to buy what we want when we want—this is the road to eternal success. Jesus said no. All these things may at times be helpful, and if they come our way through hard work, the blessing of God and the kindness of friends, let's celebrate our thankfulness and gratitude. But once these things become a goal in themselves, we become hedonistic. Pleasure should be a by-product of serving God, secondary to being a blessing to others. It is when pleasure becomes a goal in itself that it begins to elude us.

Kingdom people are not those who have retreated from the world, but those who have found they can live in it without being a part of it, enjoy it without having a permanent attachment to it, with the full understanding that this is God's world even though it is fallen.

While there was little to separate Jesus from those around him in terms of his dress, interests and daily life, it was to be found on closer inspection that his values were totally different. Kingdom people are to be a radical alternative to this world by enjoying the craftsmanship of things made by God and man, *without* making personal happiness and pleasure the aims of their lives.

3. The devil

While it is not a phrase we hear much about now, 'the devil made me do it' is still an attitude that is with us. We must face the fact that we are all morally responsible for our actions. Nobody can make us angry; it is our attitude to the person or situation that makes us angry and that keeps us angry! No one can make us resentful; it is our attitude towards the circumstances of life and those around us which makes us resentful. As moral beings living in a moral universe we will one day face a moral God and give an answer for the morality of our lives.

Passing the buck started in the Garden of Eden and is seen everywhere today between business executives and trade unions, politicians of opposing parties, family feuds

—indeed anywhere where there is human activity. But the Christian has yet another ace up his sleeve. When he can't find any human being to blame for his misdeeds, attitudes and decisions, there is always the devil!

Now when I talk about the devil, I mean all he represents in terms of the demonic world. Generally speaking for the Christian, Satan resorts to subtle temptations. He is the arch-deceiver. Sometimes he gets us to use our spiritual gifts and ministries for our own ends. If he cannot persuade us to leave what we are doing, he will allure us into building our own religious empires and make a name for ourselves. He will work on our pride to convince us that recognition with the world, even at the cost of compromise and imitation, will bring glory to God.

One of the reasons fellowship with other people is so important, is simply because deception is a terrible thing and self-deception is worst of all. We all have blind areas in our lives. I'm quite sure I haven't got any, quite simply because I can't see any! But others have a habit of pointing them out to me!

Out of control?

Jane had been a Christian for about three years. Although she'd been meeting with us regularly, many fears had been cultivated throughout her life. We have to confess that these had not been detected, or, if they had been, they weren't taken seriously. She would be gripped by fear of walking in the dark, fearful of what other people thought of her, to the point of immobility. Fearing the opposite sex as well as any talk about demons, ghosts and the unseen realms.

One evening, while worshipping, she broke down and wept. Another girl and I took her out into another room. I had an immediate sense that this was not the normal fear that most girls have at times, but that it was demonic. 'Jane, what's the trouble?' I gently enquired. There was a long silence amidst the sobbing. 'I'm afraid...afraid of everything...afraid of ghosts...talking about the occult ...the dark...anything spiritual that I cannot see...I'm even afraid of God!'

'Do you want to be free from this fear?' I asked her. She answered immediately, 'Oh yes—I'd do anything to be free of this.' I closed my eyes and quietly began to pray. (Demons are not afraid of noise!) I prayed over her generally, reminding her of God's love, and then I took authority over this spirit of fear. There was a piercing scream and I quickly looked up to find Jane bearing down on me, her face contorted, with fingers outstretched about to claw out my eyes. I had no time to think up a quick prayer! I held up my forefinger, raising myself up from the chair and spoke in tongues. Once I had gained my equilibrium, I commanded the demon, 'Out!' With that she slumped back into her chair, with all the colour coming back to her face, returning to the pretty girl she was. By now I was shaking like a leaf but endeavoured to look cool, calm and collected! We didn't quite know what to say to one another, and Carol our mutual friend looked on in astonished bewilderment, as neither of us had seen anything quite like this before. Eventually I spluttered with a measure of embarrassment, 'Are you okay, Jane?' She smiled and sighed, 'Oh yes—I'm fine now.' I tried to make a joke. 'You should have seen your face,' I quipped. With a grin she replied, 'You should have seen *yours*!'

Double protection

All of us living in this world are influenced by spirits and demons. Our walls and defences are weak in certain places; that is why we need the Holy Spirit and one another.

Being 'in Christ' and also 'in the body' of believers in the Lord Jesus should be ample protection from demonic sources. But backsliding from Christ, isolation from believers and a general sense of independence leaves us wide open to such forces. Permissiveness does precede possession, and if we permit ourselves to exaggerate and continually tell lies, we must not be surprised that a lying spirit can come and take up residence without being detected. However, a spirit will hardly take up residence where there are no open doors and no ungodly causes being deliberately cultivated.

Submitting to God is an act of the will and an attitude of the heart. Those cultivated, fear-formed attitudes of Jane's should have been confessed; then such an encounter would not have been necessary. John the apostle summed up our safety with the words, 'Greater is He who is in you than he who is in the world' (1 Jn 4:4).

Submitting to God is simply endeavouring to live the way he wants us to live: in fellowship with others; growing as we acknowledge our faults, areas of weakness and sin; getting help through the love, care, affection and truth of the Spirit and the brotherhood. This kind of relationship doesn't leave too much room for enemy activity! 'Submit therefore to God, resist the devil and he will flee from you' (Jas 4:7) is as valid today in our sophisticated twentieth century as it was in Israel 2,000 years ago.

Certainty in uncertain times

The reason the Scriptures, fellowship with others and prayer are so important is that they give us certainty in uncertain times. Far from focusing our attention on the world system, fleshly inclinations and the demonic world, we should be concentrating on expressing and enjoying the salvation that Christ has purchased for us.

It is often the unknown that people are afraid of. How will I turn out to be? What is the world coming to? Has the enemy got some foothold in my life? All these are fruitless areas of enquiry. I am extremely fulfilled and happy because I know I am loved. Both by God—which is the most wonderful thing a man can know, and by my family and friends around me. 'There is no fear in love' (1 Jn 4:18). Warfare, terrorism, mounting inflation, wholesale abortion, immorality, crime, racism, easy divorce and (strangely enough in our sophisticated age) poverty, all combine to cast lengthening shadows over our lives. They conspire to generate fear instead of love, darkness instead of light, hopelessness instead of hope. But the life God gives not only frees from fear, sin and the devil, but causes our energies to be turned round to bring blessing to the oppressed, to bring the love of Christ to those subject to social injustice.

Not only free from continual and habitual sin, but free to bless others with the blessing with which we've been blessed. That's a miracle. To bring joy to the joyless, hope to the hopeless, strength to the weak, purity to the unclean, freedom to the bound. That's the gospel!

Chapter 7

Found Out and Purged Out

To me it is becoming increasingly evident that God is not trying to change us nearly as much as we try and change ourselves. As we have already seen, he wants us to be pioneers and not settlers, to be a part of his kingdom and not settle for our own empire. He is with us to change us in those areas and many more. But the Holy Spirit wants us to grow up and realize what the gospel has *already* done for us. There is no need for further self-effort on our part, simply co-operation.

No more pretence

'Love your neighbour as yourself' (Mt 19:19) said the law. At the risk of sounding like a phrase from a well known lager advert—only the gospel can do this! It is impossible to truly love other people unless you do love yourself. People who fail to appreciate themselves find it extremely difficult to appreciate others. It is in fact an affront to the craftsmanship of God to dislike, hate, or be unthankful for the way we are.

Many people give themselves to others, not through a selfless love, but through insecurity and a low estimation of themselves. To satisfy some emotional need through their work.

Commenting on this, C. S. Lewis in one of his books said of Mrs Fidget that 'she was the sort of woman who lived for others. You could always tell the others by the hunted look on their faces!' Criticize one of these 'selfless givers' and see what happens. Such criticism will breed defensiveness. That defensiveness breeds fear. Fear breeds exclusivism, and before we know where we are walls of pretence go up which are fortified, protected and strengthened daily. Insecure people, or those with a low self-image, by the very nature of their problem tend to be closed books when it comes to relationships and friendships, even though they may have a lot to say and have colourful personalities.

Learning to be open

One of the best things that is happening among God's people at the moment is a spiritual awareness which is enabling us to see through one another. The veneer-type of relationship, consisting of a highly polished surface, is being worn through. The inferior quality of material is discovered, consisting of a web of fears, worries and concerns. Isolated individuals who spend a lot of their time pretending are a fertile sowing ground for lies from the devil. But God doesn't want us locked up to the circumstances of life and those lies. We end up destroying with our minds what God has put in our hearts, both for ourselves and others.

One woman I know of was embarrassed and insecure about the fact that she was a Christian and her husband was a typical man of the world. She engineered her way into a place of total pretence concerning the firm belief that God would redeem her husband. Having made her confession of faith, she set out to convert him. Cliff Richard records were played incessantly! Bibles and Christian books were left open on coffee tables and bedside cabinets. Even when relaxing watching television, his wife would always point out 'the born-again believer' in the programme! Of course, far from having the desired effect, it put the poor man right off.

Eventually she did the appropriate thing and shared her dilemma with some mature Christian friends. She was told quite firmly to put Cliff back in the record collection, place her Bible back in the bookshelf and stop pushing Christian literature under her husband's nose. She was told to allow him to enjoy his sport without interruption and, far from putting pressure on, find ways of taking it off! She was advised to give herself to her husband, loving and caring for him, with affection and commitment. I've no need to say that within a short while the husband's whole attitude changed.

Several months later he found out that it was in fact the leaders of the Christian group she attended who told her to change her attitude and behave towards him properly. He wanted to meet them straight away! Having been exposed to Christian leadership, teaching and friendship, he repented of living life without Christ and surrendered himself to the Lord Jesus. Talking with a Christian leader after his conversion he said, 'Being married to her was like going to bed with Billy Graham!'

It was through openness and fellowship that this woman eventually released the pressure of having to cope on her own. Of having to pretend that things were actually different from the way they were. She stopped being religious and started to live! Many of her insecurities were filled in, her concern about what others thought of her (or, more to the point, what her husband thought of her) evaporated, and she found a brand new relationship emerging. Pretence was purged out once she had been found out.

We can be assured that God loves us for who we are, not what he thinks we are! He's under no illusions. We are not supposed to cope with life on our own, but within the context of loving, open relationships, where people know us for what we really are.

There is of course emotional tension in working through honest relationships, but it is not to be compared to the turmoil created by isolation and independence. Thank God that security is not a goal within itself. The end of the Spirit-filled life is not a secure and well integrated personality. The greatest men of Bible times and modern history have not had well integrated personalities. What would it profit a man if he gained a well integrated personality and an efficiently organized empire and lost his usefulness in the kingdom of God? The chief objective of man is not an unruffled disposition, but rather to devote himself, with all the emotional traumas of life, to the government and rule of Christ. However, an increasing measure of security and integration can be expected as we live the way God wants us to live, which will be a real blessing both to God and to those around us. If we do right, God will see to it that we come out right—and this is true of all relationships.

Leave us alone!

It is impossible to be the light of the world when there is so much darkness in us (Mt 6:22–23). In these days prophets are appearing to deal with this situation. One of the reasons we don't take to the prophetic ministry emerging in the church at present, is simply because prophets and those with a prophetic ministry make us feel insecure. However, we should welcome the prophetic word, especially from friends and confirmed men of God. For God's word brings light, not darkness, life not death, enabling us to be open and known rather than motivated by fear and concern leading to an ungodly privacy.

We must always remember that the pioneer is in continual need of the prophetic, now word of God. This is not something simply for the settler or the empire builder. You can pioneer and then settle down. Or serve God and Christ's rule and then, with what you've learnt upon the way, build up your own empire. The nearer you get to Christ, and therefore become a blessing to other people, the greater threat you are to the kingdom of darkness. So temptations will not dwindle.

No individual, family, or Christian group of any sort is in a position to reject prophetic ministry. You don't have to accept everything that those who claim to be prophets are saying. We must not abandon our critical faculties. But we must be open to God and indeed expect God to speak prophetically, challenging us to further openness, holiness and usefulness. One of the reasons prophetic ministry is being challenged in these days is simply because you cannot have prophetic ministry around and remain unchanged. Experienced church people often don't want change and will challenge the prophets for this reason.

Gift and character

The more publicly gifted a person is, the more it seems there is need for discipline and accountability. In their better moments the Jewish nation did not believe that the kingdom of God would come through those who were undisciplined, unaccountable, self-seeking, deceptive, living in darkness, unrighteous, or unfaithful. As a result of giftedness there is a tendency to gather the rewards of hard work, efficient administration, plus the appreciation of others around you, shutting out Christ without whom there would be none of these things. We leave ourselves with the itch for recognition, applause, appreciation, fame or financial blessing, some of which Christ may intend for us. But not without him!

Because God is blessing us, it doesn't mean to say that we're living the way he wants us to live. It has been said that the atheist's most embarrassing moment is when he feels profoundly thankful for something, but cannot think of anybody to thank for it! Having been blessed by God it is very easy for speakers, cell group leaders, singers, youth leaders, Bible study teachers, clergy—indeed those in any form of responsibility—to overplay their importance in God's purposes and eventually become the centre of things. God is pushed out of the centrality of life and something or someone else emerges to take his place. That something then becomes an idol. More room is then given to our idol, which of course we want God to bless and recognize, than to God himself.

So we must not be deceived into thinking that God's blessing in our own life and ministry is necessarily a result of his rule. If God can bless the atheist, he can certainly bless the born-again believer, especially a very gifted one, without changing his character.

One of the basics of a godly character is a teachable spirit. Jesus was continually being taught, led and directed by his heavenly Father. He did not have it all sewn up, simply drawing on his own resources (see Jn 5:19).

Some people never realize and explore their gift. They live right in the centre of a wide circle, never moving out to the boundaries that God has placed around them. They always live within their safe areas where they will never have to make any mistakes or make a fool of themselves. There are others of course who not only live near the boundaries, but often go miles beyond them. But anybody with any form of public ministry will have to face the fact that if they allow themselves continually to be drawn out in that area it will be to the detriment of their character.

Frankly, I am amazed that men with enormous character deficiencies, who are neither admitting to them nor asking for help in them, are regularly asked to speak, plan, administrate or minister in some way for major Christian events. Theologically we subscribe to the fact that character is more important than gift, but in reality it seems to work the other way round. We are so keen to get the job done, we fail to see that character formation is the foundation upon which our gifts operate to get the job done. On the basis that we reproduce after our own likeness, we could be in severe trouble in ten years' time—unless those in public ministry are made more accountable in what they say and do.

Kingdom authority

All people are gifted. Therefore all of us need to be under authority. We need to be helped, for example, to discover whatever usefulness we have. If we are continually stretching beyond that sphere we will create for ourselves a hopeless insecurity complex.

I used to think there was a serious misprint in the Bible. I was utterly convinced that the centurion with the sick servant should have said that a man *in* authority has authority. This I failed to understand. It is of course exactly as he stated: the man *under* authority has authority (Mt 8:9). When a Roman soldier gave a command, disobedience meant you were referred back to the Sergeant at Arms. Further disobedience would have referred you back to the Centurion, then the Commander of the force, and theoretically at least, even to Caesar himself! The soldier who was *under* authority potentially had the authority of the entire Roman army at his disposal. Sadly those who make a lot of their authority are not actually under any authority in God's eyes. Protestants have fought to do away with the Pope, but have replaced him in the local church and para-church organizations with dozens of little popes all heading up their own little empires. 'Resist the devil and he will flee from you—resist the deacons and they will fly at you' is still sadly true!

But church, we are being found out! People are beginning to see through the veneer. Our authority is being questioned—and about time too! It is only the man who is truly *under* authority who is *in* authority. Leadership is not a matter of promotion but of function. It isn't even a permanent gift. When a person has finished his sphere of leadership and usefulness he should gladly step back into some other sphere. Uselessness in one sphere does not mean uselessness in every sphere. There are multitudes of 'leaders' throughout Britain whose usefulness, as leaders, disappeared years ago. Yet they still have to carry out their duties, clinging onto their roles, exercising authority but not actually being under authority. Many of these men are not actually exercising authority: all they are doing is continually establishing, re-establishing and re-re-establishing an authority. It becomes very wearing for all involved.

It is a sad fact that the most regimented denominations and non-denominations are run by those who are actually under no authority whatever. The so-called pyramid systems, where everybody is under somebody else, has got one major flaw. The person at the top isn't under anybody! As far as I'm concerned what's good for the man at the top is good for everybody else all the way down. When a friend of mine was asked if he was in the 'pyramid system' he replied, 'I really don't know what you mean. There aren't any pyramids in Israel, they are all in Egypt!'

Giving permission

Every now and then I gather my friends together and we sit down and chat through what they feel my strengths and weaknesses are. At times it hurts, but most of the time it is a tremendous encouragement to get on and do what I can do well. We need continually to be giving each other authority to say what is appropriate and necessary. It gives a wonderful sense of security and enables us to function within our gift, whether it is public or apparently low key. One of the best ways of dealing with criticism is to know that there is a group of people around you who love you enough to be honest and truthful. That way you don't have to listen to every comment, jibe and negative remark that is made by those around us.

This mutual submission wonderfully develops our character, turning us away from selfish individualism and defensive attitudes. It enables us to respect the insights of others. Giving others authority is one of the major steps towards exercising our own authority. Of course in the end we've all only got as much authority as we are given, and to try to make more than that is ill advised and unhelpful. God has given us authority to serve him and those around us. Those in authority are not worth more than those who look to them for authority. It's simply a matter of function, not status.

Those who hold office, but have no real authority through respect of who they are in God, will be found out. They will be seen to be something other than kingdom people. Those to whom God has given authority must continually allow every vestige of superiority to be purged out, refraining from using people as fodder for their own evangelical/charismatic purposes.

The new sectarianism

It is very strange, but nevertheless true, that when there is a new mood about, some of us can change our liturgy while at heart remaining the same as we've always been. In recent years a new brand of extra-local fellowship life has emerged which has been encouraging and yet disappointing. Vast sections of the body of Christ are being enriched by a fresh quality of life, community, expressive worship and praise, breaking down the sacred and secular, life-oriented rather than service/meeting-oriented.

However, things are not always as they appear to be. And the cloistered emphasis, along with a general super-religious attitude to things, still pervades what is currently known as the house-church and charismatic movements.

In many cases these groups have become a network of, in the main, like-minded people, linked together, generally to the detriment of other believers of differing persuasions in the locality.

I happen to believe that it is important that emerging groups go through a kind of strategic introversion. Many of us have been taught that 'identity precedes function' and any new fellowship or grouping would do well to find their identity together before they get too involved in evangelism and church growth.

Yet it needs to be underlined that there is a tremendous richness in God's kingdom which we all need. We are going to have to adopt an altered state of consciousness if we are to be taken out of authoritarian, like-minded groups. It is a fact that continual inter-breeding creates deformity and weakness in the physical realm, and it's no different in the spiritual realm.

In the short term a local fellowship may be blessed, strengthened, fed and matured by the small team of 'related men' and ministries. But in the long term all we shall see are loads of isolated circles headed up by various 'apostles' where a healthy overlap becomes almost impossible. The government of God, as Ezekiel saw it, was 'as if one wheel were within another wheel' or circles within circles (Ezek 10:10). God has no problem with circles, providing they are not exclusive circles. We all tend to move within circles of friendships, but these are to be overlapping, allowing God to add others to us and us to others.

I want to make it quite clear that I believe in apostolic ministry. It is one of the things being restored to the church today. That is not to say that everybody who says he is an apostle actually is an apostle. But neither is it true to say that everyone who says he is a pastor is a pastor! We do rather tend to get paranoid about prophets and apostles, while we have loads of pastors who can't shepherd, evangelists who bring few to Christ and Bible teachers who have never read the Bible through even once!

Apostles and prophets are given by God to the church to lay foundations, give direction, and keep redeemed communities on course. But it seems that the most gifted men are often the most insecure. It is a pity that some of these men need continually to administrate people, fellowships and organizations under their wing, to give visible backing and clout to their ministry. We are in a day when many local churches are seeing their need of covering and accountability, especially where bishops, area superintendents and denominational heads may be either unregenerate or unsympathetic to change. So 'apostles' are called in to help. On occasion they offer their services or imply that they need to be called in! Involvement with such an apostolic covering almost invariably involves the leadership of a local fellowship in a certain circle of conferences, weekends, public meetings and leadership groups. But increasingly one discovers that these apostles, with few exceptions, are only interested in what *they* are doing and what those associated with them are doing. There is not an outright denial of the grace of God in other circles, or denominations, rather an attitude of, 'You do the Lord's work your way, and we'll do it his!'

One of the obvious dangers of this tunnel-vision mentality is that all the fellowships under a particular 'apostle' look the same. In the early church some fellowships observed sabbath days and some certainly did not. Others were somewhat fussed by what they ate, others certainly were not. But not so today. If an 'apostle' says head coverings are to be worn, in the name of submission and obedience all those fellowships wear head coverings. It is of course necessary to attend *his* conferences, leaders' weekends and special events, and no others!

If we replace a traditional denominational outlook which has a low level of spirituality with a new, exciting, but still denominational outlook which has a higher level of spirituality, we do not have much to do with God's ultimate intentions. It is simply a better quality of empire.

Living in the presence of unearthly powers, God is calling us to find one another in true fellowship, standing together against all evil, even the evil of sectarianism—to the glory of God. This altered state of consciousness, far from impoverishing our lives, will enrich them enormously. It is true that some platforms in Britian are so open they couldn't hold a *conviction* between them, but it has to be said that many of the newer groupings with their own annual conferences and weekends are so closed they couldn't hold a *contradiction* between them! Learning to live with our differences in kingdom life is a major part of what God is calling us to today.

The sight of seeing men working together, with long term relationships, will be the miracle of all ages. God wants to keep us from hiving off to do our own little thing, however large it may appear to us. Replacing the old system with a new system just gives a more enjoyable system to live in.

I do have some sympathy with the newer fellowships that have emerged with what, to my mind, is an over-strong, overbearing attitude to authority. Run by men who, as I have said before, are often under no authority themselves. It is a reaction to the total lack of shepherding, discipleship and discipline in most churches throughout the United Kingdom. It is therefore very unwise for many of the traditional denominations to criticize the new movements when there is such an obvious 'don't you tell me what to do' attitude among many in their own congregations.

But if we don't come out of a sectarian system, it will not be long before the sectarian system comes out in us!

Learning from our roots

Israel was unlike any other nation. It had no central government and there were no class distinctions. It was simply a loose federation of clans. It is this loose-knit, relatively flexible arrangement that the Holy Spirit is after today. The kingdom is founded on Christ and is to be expressed through a loose-knit, but nevertheless related, committed, covenant-keeping people. At present, some churches have specific relationships with men to the exclusion of general relationships. Others have general relationships but nothing specific. We need both!

We need to rediscover that the kingdom is built on a relationship with God and one another which is not based purely on function. Some wish to function together without relating to each other, but God wants it the other way round. First we learn to relate together, and then we tackle what God gives us to *do* together. But more of that in the next chapter.

Closed-minded groups, including many of the newer ones, will not only be sectarian but will also fail to produce creative energy. And where there are people who want to relate to these newer groupings, without coming 'under their covering' as it is called, they will find it almost impossible. The result may be very much better than historic churches in terms of the quality of life together. But in the long term it will be found out that sectarianism, superiority—and perhaps fear of doing things differently —will have to be purged out.

There will of course be the few who will follow conscience and dare to do what their 'authority' would disapprove of. Long live courageous men!

Chapter 8

Friends! Friends! Friends!

Friendship lasts for ever—and if the friendships we are forming now are not going to count in the age to come, then much of what we are doing in this time-space world is a complete waste of time. It is lunacy to imagine that we are not going to know anybody but Jesus in the age to come, walking around with no identity, names or distinguishing features! We *are* going to know one another in the age to come. Yes, it will be different; it will be better!

We have been given to each other to nourish and sustain, bless and influence, correct and adjust, motivate and appreciate. God has given us to the people we like, not to possess them but to honour, esteem, enjoy and serve them in any way we can.

A relaxed evening among friends, when we can truly be ourselves without any pretence, is a rich privilege, but it is one that God intends.

Most Christians are too busy to have real friends, especially the 'out and out' ones. 'I have come that you may have meetings, and that you may have them more abundantly.' The reason many believers are out and out is quite simply because they are never in—they are always at meetings!

Many church structures, meetings, offices and responsibilities actually destroy friendships and families. Jesus, however, laid tremendous emphasis on friendships. 'No longer do I call you slaves . . . but I have called you friends' (Jn 15:15).

Business before pleasure?

Jesus not only had friends, he had a best friend called John. Peter and James were close runners-up! The Bible tells us that at one time Jesus had 500 disciples. Within that group he had seventy, and among the seventy were found to be twelve special followers. Within the twelve there were three, and even within that three there was what the Authorized Version of the Bible calls 'the other disciple whom Jesus loved' (Jn 20:2). He obviously favoured John more than the others, and he favours some today more than others. You may say to me, 'Jesus hasn't got any favourites!' Well, that is perhaps because you are not one of them! Some people please Jesus more than others.

It is quite astounding, in the light of our own church activity and the way we do things, that Jesus is never recorded as having spent time alone with Judas. Most of us are far too busy spending our time with the difficult, unlovely, the time-consumers and the selfish, to spend any time with folk we like! One of the reasons Christians in responsibility often look so tired, harassed and weary is simply because they spend most of their time with people they do not like. True, the gospel encourages us to love the unlovely and to give ourselves to those who are lonely, but not to the exclusion of developing carefree, enriching friendships.

Built together

God is after an army of friends. Much of our feverish

activity and churchianity has got to be wound down in order for us to truly become friends. To spend time with one another, eating, drinking, sharing life, praying and finding one another. Fellowship is not hymn singing or Bible study, house decorating or gardening together; it is when we find one another, when we walk in the light. We cannot be light to the world when there is so much darkness in our relationships together as the people of God.

As we have already seen, corporately in our local fellowships we may have to go through a strategic period of introversion. Jesus will then give us something to do with our newly established friendships. He is not after an exclusive bless-me club, but he does want us to work together, wherever possible, on a foundation of deep, open relationships.

Many of the new fellowships which have emerged in Britain over the last ten years need to face the fact that friendship is not an end in itself. It is not a goal. God wants to energize those friendships so that we can give ourselves away and be a blessing to others both inside and outside the kingdom.

But God is not simply after an army; it is to be an army of *friends*. Our activity, strategy and usefulness is to be based on friendship. In the end it is not the strategy that will see us through, but our friendships, the relationships that God has given us. That way, whether we have anything to do or not we will be found together, worshipping, blessing and honouring our God.

Of late, I've been involved in several 'committees' of one sort or another. Most of these are together purely on the basis of getting a job done—locally or nationally. Take away the project and most of those brothers would never see anything of each other again. There is no relationship, no real friendship. In fact quite often these working relationships are made up of public politeness and private contempt. Men working together, who behind the scenes have little genuine respect, time or enjoyment of one another. This is not what God is after.

Open friendships

Besides my wife Anona, there are a number of friends who know almost everything there is to know about me. If there are any details I haven't told them I'd be willing to share those as well. I can't tell you what a relief it is. It means, quite simply, that I can be myself on and off the platform, whether among friends or enemies, working or relaxing. There is nothing they will ever find out about me that will shock or surprise them. So they don't love me for what they think I am, but rather for what they *know* I am. This has reduced me to tears on several occasions. In my better moments I realize I am not worthy of such love and commitment, never mind faithfulness.

Of course we cannot love everybody in the same way. God gives us the right to choose our friends and at what level we wish to relate. But many of us, especially leaders, are ensnared in a network of obligatory relationships.

Even as the main leader of our community in Cobham, I rarely visit anyone other than close friends. I like to think that friendships involve those people *we* choose, whereas fellowship involves those people *God* chooses us to relate to.

A. W. Tozer, author and prophet, although titled 'pastor' was blatantly everything but a pastor. He was well aware of this fact, and rarely visited anybody in his congregation. On one occasion he felt he really ought to visit one of his elders who had been taken sick and was now in hospital. Upon entering the room, the elder was so shocked to see Tozer doing a pastoral visit that he sat bolt upright in bed and declared, 'I'm not that sick!'

Tozer had chosen his friends and was not under the pressure of doing professional rounds, pretending to be everybody's friend. Men who simply hide behind ministry are rarely known by anybody at the end of the day, leaving them open to all sorts of attacks from the enemy.

The way forward

I thank God for prompting me to share my life with others. I've been able to express my hopes, fears, dreams; talk about things that cause me to flip my lid, shout with praise, dance, or cry; things that cause me to become selfish and depressed and to fail the Lord. Those people know my financial situation, sexual weaknesses, plus the areas in which I am easily intimidated. However, such relationships are rare and are not easily found. But there are some things we can do to make room for them if we want them.

I've noticed that most relationships tend to go through three stages.

1. Veneer

This is the stage where we are nicer than God himself. Even God isn't as nice as most Christians! It is the highly polished stage.

Of course the only way we can get to know each other is through the impression we leave with each other. Most of us like to impress, irrespective of whether or not we have the wherewithal to do so. The difficulty is that we give the impression that we are solid gloss and shine all the way through. I must admit I am very wary of such people. There is of course nothing wrong with veneer-type relationships. We live with them every day as we go about business and meet people in shops, on our doorsteps, etc.

The real sadness comes when we never get beyond that stage with people who know and love the Lord Jesus, people we have known for years.

The point is well illustrated by a story I heard recently about a friend of mine who fell through the floor of his fashionable house. Wood-boring beetles had eaten through the timber. But as it turns out, wood-boring beetles don't like polish. So on the surface everything looked well, but underneath were decay and danger!

If we are going to have relationships of value, worth and stability, we must get beyond this veneer stage.

2. *Disillusionment*

A friend of mine called Charles visited Cliff Richard on one occasion. Cliff and he chatted for a while, with Cliff perched on a long, beautiful, marble-onyx coffee table. Cliff went out to make some coffee and Charles sat where Cliff had just been seated. Within moments there was an almighty crack like a gunshot. Charles' weight (considerably greater than Cliff's) did a thorough job. Being of solid material, it was simply re-cut into two sections; the sides were re-polished and four more legs later Cliff was the proud owner of two marble coffee tables!

However, most wooden furniture has a superior finish —it is called veneer. Below the shiny surface is an inferior-quality material. Knock a corner off your coffee table and you will see what I mean. Unless they told you in the store that it was solid mahogany, you wouldn't be surprised to find a cheaper-quality material underneath.

When it comes to relating we do tend to view people as though they are almost flawless, unless we have taken an instant disliking to them. Then when we get to know them we find their insecurities, defence mechanisms, critical attitudes, plain unfaithfulness and downright selfishness

—just like ourselves! Surprised, hurt, shocked and disillusioned we then give that person a wide berth and pick up another relationship. When it happens to us again with that person, we drop them (in the nicest possible way of course) and start off again with someone else. Live like that for a few years in a local fellowship and the church would be full of 'nice' but fractured relationships.

There is a lot of unfaithfulness around in the church. What I have described is a sort of spiritual fornication or adultery—though there is not much about it that is very spiritual. This foundation of evasive action, putting things under the carpet, and plain selfishness, is no foundation upon which to build a loving community. We must face disillusionment.

3. Opt out or choose reality

There is a lovely story about a traveller who was looking for the living God. On his travels, feeling he was nearing his destination, he enquired the way. A native pointed across some barren terrain. 'That is where your living God lives,' he said firmly. Our traveller friend then turned his head in another direction, and instantly saw a beautiful city, filled with colour, music and happy noises. 'Well what is that?' he said, pointing to the city. 'Oh—that is God City,' replied the native. 'I thought you said God lived over there, across that rugged territory,' said the traveller. 'He does,' confirmed the native. 'Then why is that called God City?' the traveller questioned. 'Ah,' said the native, somewhat embarrassed. 'You see—those city dwellers were also once travellers. They were looking for the living God as well. But when they found out that he lives across that rugged, open plain, they settled here, on this side, and built a city which they named after God.'

Those looking for God among their friends often discover where he is. They then have to go through the rugged and rough terrain of the pain of being known and knowing others. Commitment, loyalty, faithfulness, self-lessness, serving one another and seeking to be a continual source of blessing, are not without their cost. It is invariably a rough terrain! We are cursed with a desire for an easy life, getting what we can, and are therefore continually tempted to take a short cut and build a city of veneer-type relationships with all the colour and razzmatazz that superficial friendships allow.

We can go through the veneer stage, get disillusioned and opt out, going straight back into another superficial relationship if we wish. Or we can allow our relationships to wear thin, pressing through the veneer of existing friendships, allowing ourselves to become disillusioned, and then recommitting ourselves to each other *in that disillusionment.* It is often necessary to take a couple of steps back, making room for God and giving one another space to breathe. But we only step back in order to go on, to develop a relationship with the love and respect it deserves, not to drop one another. If we allow ourselves the luxury of illusions about friends, we are bound to become *dis*illusioned sooner or later. So let's choose reality.

Making room for God

Conflict is the essence of drama. As we are a part of God's unfolding drama across the earth, conflict must therefore be expected, embraced and worked through. Superficial 'God City' is the only alternative.

It is therefore becoming increasingly clear that almost every issue we have in the church is basically one of relationships. Behind every so-called 'personality' or 'doctrinal' conflict is an issue of righteousness and unrighteousness. It is one thing to be filled with the Spirit as an individual, but quite another to be joined to others of varying cultures, backgrounds and temperaments in a practical day-to-day experience. If we are to be God's alternative society, we shall have to find out how to get on with one another. I do not mean how to put up with one another, but how to live with one another in a sharing, caring, vulnerable, honest community.

Triangle lifestyles

The importance of close friendships and community is becoming obvious. Most people live in triangles. They work in A, live in B, and worship in C. Neighbours rarely see us because we are either at work or church. The church rarely sees us because we are either at work or at home. Those in business have no idea of where we live or how we go to church. This is a sort of church-on-wheels where nobody in one area knows how the other areas operate. It is difficult bringing Christ's lordship into those situations. If of course the local church we are in gets too noisy, quiet, charismatic, or boring, such a situation allows us to change churches with ease, as relationships hardly come into it. The church in the locality simply becomes a matter of convenience rather than commitment.

The playboy philosophy of 'get what you can from a fellowship and when you have drained it dry and it can give you no more, move on' has been adopted by far too many. If a church gets too hot, drop it. If people dislike you, clear off. Never get too involved, never get hurt. Run your life the way you want it run and use your friends to satisfy your needs. This playboy philosophy has brought dishonour to the gospel and shame to the name of Christ.

Of course Christ does not want inordinate loyalty. Men committed to men without Christ standing between them is horrible. But that is hardly the situation in the church in Britain at present.

Relationships, it needs to be said, are not some sort of endurance test. There are occasions when it is good not to continue a relationship for a while. Sometimes friction makes it wise to withdraw by mutual consent, until God is able to bring about harmony and put the pieces back together again. However, there is a difference between withdrawing from fellowship in order to give God room and time to mend things, and withdrawing to break fellowship due to faithlessness.

When Anona and I were married we exchanged rings. These were not only a token of our love but also of an agreed commitment and exclusive attachment. It is not emotion that has kept our marriage together; it is this commitment based upon a moral foundation. Bonhoeffer writing to his niece commented, 'It is not love that will keep your marriage alive, but marriage that will keep your love alive.'

Eventually Anona and I had a rough patch in our relationship. We became disillusioned with each other. We had let down our defences, gone through the 'they can do no wrong' stage and then discovered things about each other which we didn't like.

It is at this stage that either party can allow stray emotional impulses to latch onto other people. To find emotional security and acceptance among others to the exclusion of one's partner is dangerous and positively harmful. So we went away for a weekend and recommitted ourselves to each other. We purchased another couple of rings and seven years after our initial commitment was made, reaffirmed our covenant, our agreement to be faithful to one another, by another exchange of rings.

Commitment couched in affection, kingdom truth and honesty will take God's purposes on in leaps and bounds.

When we commit ourselves to others for the purpose of convenience it will initially look good and be emotionally satisfying, but in the long run it won't last and will be seen for what it really is. A covenant-keeping God can only be seen among a covenant-keeping people, and an agreement-keeping God wishes to express his morality through an agreement-keeping people. We are Christ's representatives, so our actions speak louder than his words.

In the age to come we shall know one another. The friendships we build now will have worth and value then. Knowing that this is but a glimpse, a vague insight into what God has in store for us throughout eternity, makes it all worth while—doesn't it! Hearing it like this we need to understand that friendships must never become an end in themselves but be used by God in his own way and time, to enrich others and draw them into our circle of influence, love and kindness. While being appreciative of what we have in terms of friendships, I believe that we should understand that God wants to give us away to a dark age where forgiveness and salvation have yet to be tasted. If that is what friendship can do—then long live friendship!

Chapter 9

Eight Reasons Why Fellowships Level Off—or Collapse

'Don't let worry kill you off—let the church help!' the garish poster declared in all innocence. I smiled—it was far too near the truth for me to do anything else.

Of course there will always be problems in life, but they should be the problems *of* life. 'We'll always have problems in life,' mused my Irish friend. 'We are meant to be a generation of overcomers, and if there are no problems, there will be nothing to overcome!' Irish wit and wisdom indeed, shot through with a good dose of spiritual sanity, I fancy.

But so many of the problems we encounter in our local church/fellowship have got nothing to do with life. They are the problems of dead churches, immovable fellowships, complete with dull, dead, boring services and meetings. Predictable to the nth degree. Such churches levelled off years ago and, were it not for the permanent structures holding everything together, they would have collapsed.

What are the main reasons for churches levelling off or collapsing? I've listed eight. To me they are the most important aspects of our shared life together, which need to be grasped, embraced and worked out. Of course without the Holy Spirit and the sense of his prompting and leading it will all be a waste of time, swapping one set of principles for another lot. But with his help we can come off our plateaux and begin to climb to the heights. Our shared life together will then be a wonderful presence and power in our locality, a magnificent backdrop for the proclamation of the gospel.

1. No foundations

God cannot build on the rubble of our past experience. Neither is it his intention to build on our accumulation of mere knowledge, however biblical it may be. Poisonous roots of deception, superiority, defensiveness, individualism and professionalism must be dug out.

When Christians fall from a healthy spiritual life, exposing shaky foundations, it is generally over one of three issues. Pride, money, or sex. These folk feel that they are God's answer for all the ills within the church, or deal dishonestly with financial rewards, or use their status to satisfy sexual desires. These three areas have caused the crash of many anointed men and women of God.

We should be concerned at the growing number of people who are travelling our nation, telling us how to run our churches, build relationships, live pure lives and be of service to the Lord by evangelizing the nation, who themselves are unapproachable, are known by nobody, do not even attend a church let alone be accountable to one, and through their travels are able to hide behind a 'ministerial' professional façade. Such people invariably have within their foundations poisonous roots which are fed by success, crowds, and a measure of fame and applause.

God is wanting to build, and a good builder always builds on firm foundations. There must be no weeds or roots left to grow and eventually crack up those foundations. Many of the things contained in the early chapters of this book deal with this aspect of kingdom living.

The house of the Lord must be built upon a righteous foundation, one which is firm and secure. I am not here talking about doctrinal foundations, but living foundations! Foundations that are clean, honest characters, open to God and wanting only to do the things that please the Lord Jesus. That is why relationships are important. They enable us to be loved and known for who we are. We no longer have to cover up or deceive when we have allowed God to build his character and quality of life into the warp and woof of our being. To build on anything else is tantamount to building the Houses of Parliament on plasticine.

The surest foundation is an overwhelming sense and knowledge of God's grace. An outright conviction that it is in his heart only to forgive, to extend mercy, and to love us. It is as we have this continual awareness of God's deep love and personal care that we can deal with our weaknesses, secure in God's everlasting tenderness.

2. No direction

Ask the average church where it is going and at best you will hear stories of an enlarged youth work, growing Sunday school, brighter meetings, perhaps a building extension or strategic, prayerful visitation programme. It may be some spectacular healing, or plans to attend one of the large festivals or conferences that have sprung up in recent years. But none of that tells you where the church is going. Blessings there may be, and plans to grow are fine, but the issue is: where is all this heading!

The church that knows where it is going is made up of people who know where they are going. Everything we say and do should be evaluated in the light of our goal. A well painted bulls-eye is easier to hit, but some have no target at all.

It is vital that we listen to the prophetic voice that is emerging among God's people. Prophetic direction, the encouragement to move on in faith, and setting God-given goals, will keep our paths straight and save us from travelling in perennial circles. Once we are moving forward we will find how much easier it is to redirect a moving object than a stationary one.

So often the church lacks direction because we concentrate our building on the wrong things. We devote our energies to the wrong areas. For instance, some fight to build inside a denomination, some outside, but it is not so much a matter of 'stay in' or 'come out', but rather 'go on' or 'go back'. We must be willing to do *anything* that will take us forward in God, preferably in the relationships we already enjoy. I believe God is speaking to the church at the moment, that we need his direction, and that this often comes from the prophets. In Old Testament times the priests ministered daily at the altar, acting as a go-between, between God and the people. Living day by day, hand to mouth, they often failed to observe that sin was creeping into God's people, with unfaithfulness and idolatry. The corrupt status quo became the norm—until the prophetic voice, giving God's direction, spoke up.

This was often not a negative voice, but one of positive commitment from God to his people—declaring, urging and inviting them to repent, change their attitude and find fresh direction as individuals, families and a community. We need direction, and we need prophets!

3. *Authority—not based on relationships*

I once saw a marvellous cartoon of a newly appointed minister speaking to his governing church body. 'Well, as the new man here,' he opened up, 'I want to say that I am bringing an end to democracy. From now on this fellowship will be run on the basis of a theocracy. And my name is—Theo!' In Britain there are very few men who actually do have their way in things—perhaps because of their governing bodies, or democratic systems of voting, or their insecurities and fears of being labelled 'dictators'.

Recently I attended a meeting where there were a number of ministers who were being questioned about their experiences in the ministry. Their stories were not confined to ecclesiastical circles and could just as easily be applied to the new forms of leadership emerging outside institutional churches today. As the evening progressed the hollowness of their answers began to show. My heart grew heavier, and at the end of the time I quietly slipped out and sat in my car and almost involuntarily uttered, 'No authority and no friends!' To have no authority but to have many friends would be one thing; to have complete authority but no friends would be something as well; but to have no authority and no friends—is it any wonder that the church is in such a mess?

The system of moving men around from parish to parish or pulpit to pulpit has had a devastating effect on the church (though sometimes it brings happy relief!). In the early church the leadership grew up from within its ranks, only rarely drawing in men to help who were not brought up in the local community. Today things are quite different. Almost inevitably the main leader has come in from elsewhere. After the initial honeymoon period and the first two or three years are over, he is either seen as the saviour of the locality and is submitted to blindly, or, as often happens, he is seen for what he is, a man with feet of clay. It isn't long before everybody else on the governing board feels he is equal with the minister. It is only a few short years before the man is looking for another post.

God has placed authority within all bodies of believers.

That authority is given by God and should be exercised by those who have received it, to serve the redeemed community and cause them to grow up in Christ. If those with that anointing and authority fail to exercise it, those with no authority and anointing will move in and take their place.

In the realm of true relationships it isn't long before we find there are many areas where we can gladly submit to one another. I am tripping over people to whom I feel I can give authority to lead me on in one way or another. It may be communicating, dealing with problems, house maintenance, or teaching me to cope with the new era of technology that is now upon us. I've been helped with Bible study, interpretation, and even fashion! The list is endless. How strange that some people feel there is nobody they can genuinely submit to, even though they might be part of a company of a hundred or more believers. Such men and women are not only common, but usually have accomplished very little in terms of building relationships of any lasting value. The main reason is that they are far too superior or insecure in their own estimation to do anything, and build selfish or condescending relationships which are short lived.

God is after communities in which there is authority based upon genuine recognition. We seem to be prepared to accept authority in other areas of life, in business, commerce, the legal profession and local government, but we find it so difficult among God's people. However, the Holy Spirit is wanting to blow away all the myths and fantasies that surround those in authority in the world, and teach us to submit to people because they are worth it, not because of their annual income, size of office, blue uniform or any other reason.

The idea of a minister, youth leader, or group leader having to *keep* people together when most of those people are not willing to submit their lives to that person is lunacy. We should be teaching people that a submissive attitude is one of the hallmarks of spirituality. Submission and obedience are different, inasmuch as submission is an attitude, whereas obedience is the result of that attitude. We are not asked to obey our leaders willy-nilly, but we are asked to submit to them in the fear of the Lord, and unless they are immoral, obedience would be the natural outcome of our attitude towards them.

We need to be *giving* people authority to direct, shape and adjust us as well as encourage, feed and nurture us. When Jesus sent his disciples out, he said, 'Do this, take this, do not do this and do not take that, go here but do not go there. If you are received, do this and if you are not received, do that.' When they returned rejoicing in the miracles they had seen, he told them they were rejoicing in the wrong things. 'Don't rejoice in this, rejoice in that.' (See Lk 10:3–11.) 'Ah, but that was Jesus,' you may say. 'He was special.' But that is not how the early disciples saw Jesus. They did not see him as we see him. They did not understand all the theological, doctrinal and historical aspects of Christ's birth, life, death, resurrection and ascension. To them he was a man who was worth submitting to. Of course none of us equals Jesus, but he reckons others are worthy of some authority. But *others* have to recognize that. We should not be telling others. When all is said and done, we have only got the authority that people give to us.

4. *When those with responsibility cease to share their hearts*

There is within the church a carpet mentality. I once belonged to a fellowship where for over thirty years people had swept under the carpet issues they were unwilling to face one another with. Eventually, of course, despite a somewhat bumpy walk on the carpet, protrusions began to show! And, of course, it is at the point of the protrusions that the problems are seen for what they are. At that stage you either have to go and buy another carpet to cover everything up, or roll it back and face what is underneath. The longer it is left down, the more difficult it becomes to roll it back.

The church does not need a new carpet. When those of any measure of maturity and responsibility cease to share the way they see things, it is in fact the beginning of the end. Life becomes a network of pretence. We simply say what's expected of us. We are more concerned with eliciting an emotional response than earning respect through our truthfulness, honesty and integrity. I am not advocating rude, insensitive behaviour from know-it-alls who feel their opinions matter more than everybody else's. But God would redirect people who set a course of unfaithfulness by continually evading issues they see in people's lives. That way an appalling lack of faithfulness can emerge, the results of which are tragic.

If we fail to share what is in our hearts, eventually we invite the kind of confrontation we had hoped to avoid. Being a fairly sensitive and intuitive person, I remember picking up some things I was unhappy about in a friend. I kept telling myself they did not matter, but all the time those things ate away at me. What eats us is sometimes more important than what we eat! After successfully (and I thought spiritually!) containing all of my reservations, concerns and annoyances about this man, he appeared on my doorstep to confront me with some difficulties he had with me! Having pointed out the areas in which he felt I needed help and adjustment, I found it impossible not to retaliate by dragging out all I had put under the carpet for two or three months! Of course the result was total confusion, and others had to come in to unscramble it.

5. Inflexible structures

Jesus knew that after harvest, presses would extract the juice from the grapes before being placed in goatskin bottles. In the time that followed, fermentation took place. Carbon dioxide produced pressure on the wineskin and, to avoid an explosion, the gas was released, another flexible container found, and the wine re-poured. After use the original goatskin became inflexible and unable to adjust to what was going on inside. The process was repeated over and over again, with the goatskin being stretched to the point where it eventually became totally inflexible.

Even after several re-pourings, the wine was still not fit for drinking. Good wine matures with time, and in the continual re-pouring, the impurities and sediment were removed and the old goatskin discarded.

The Holy Spirit is on a collision course with all forms of inflexible Christianity. So to those who are keen to have new wine in their localities, watch your goatskins! If you try to maintain the new wine in an old inflexible wineskin, eventually there will be an explosion (though it may take years), and then you lose the wine as well as the goatskin!

6. Prolonged discouragement

God rarely uses a discouraged person. Because of some of the issues already mentioned, entire congregations can slip into periods of prolonged discouragement. Sometimes this comes because the leadership or the more vocal parties of a Christian community set unreal expectations. We tend to put our faith in men, procedures and programmes, and when they fail us we become discouraged. It is important we set ourselves *realistic* goals so that our expectations are on a similar level.

Generally speaking, when a church looks as though it's had an overdose of Horlicks, it doesn't need volleys of condemnatory remarks, further pressure and fresh standards. What it probably needs is a jolly good dose of encouragement! It is important we find out what God *is* doing and start with that, rather than continually highlighting what *isn't* happening and majoring on that. We can only work with what we've got, both in terms of people and resources, and it's vital that we learn to encourage and nurture what there is.

There are those who have what is called the ministry of encouragement. God has gifted them in ways whereby, simply being what they are, continual encouragement flows to others. We need to release these people in such situations, to draw our attention away from our own personal circumstances and the disappointments of corporate church life—and direct our vision to the Lord and what he is doing.

The alternative is to believe for the worst and prepare for no change. It's rather like the hypochondriac who had engraved on his tombstone, 'I told you so!'

Encouragement creates hope where there was hopelessness. Words and actions contain spiritual power to build faith or destroy it. Encouragement also deals with rejection. There are times when we all feel rejected or out of things. People need to feel loved, important and a bit special. A fellowship where there is a lack of encouragement makes sad the city of God, but encouragement revitalizes the spirit.

In seeking to be a blessing to God and those around us, we can become tired and exhausted. We lose the ability to laugh. I remember the words of Malcolm Muggeridge when he was interviewed on a television chat-show. 'I suppose we need more sincere people in leadership,' mused the interviewer. 'My dear boy,' responded

Malcolm, 'we don't need any more sincere people in the world. Hitler was sincere! We need people in leadership who can laugh at themselves. Once you've lost the ability to laugh, you become insane. Look at all the world's dictators; very few of them have a sense of humour, and even fewer are able to laugh at themselves.' Leadership, power, authority and at times overwhelming responsibilities all conspire to drain laughter from us. But it is important, and what is more, highly therapeutic, that we cultivate the ability to laugh. And what is more, laugh at ourselves.

That is why small cell groups are important. They enable us to be known, loved and encouraged for who we are, and also help us to have a good laugh at ourselves. Such relationships cause us to be less sensitive and selfish.

7. *Slave mentality*

Speaking on the issue of slavery, Abraham Lincoln once said, 'If ever I get a chance to hit that thing, I'll hit it hard!' To me there is something worse than physical and social slavery, and that is religious slavery. Wherever the church has become an instrument of bondage, binding the minds and hardening the hearts, it opposes its own gospel.

The differences between a slave society and a free society lie in the number of free acts possible in each. In a closed, totalitarian society, central government make as many decisions as possible, leaving society to make as few as possible. The free, democratic society should work on the basis of central government making as few decisions as possible, allowing society to make as many as possible. That is how it should work anyway! God loves to see his creation making moral choices and enjoying the benefits of those choices.

There are of course moral qualities of life which the

church must endeavour to absorb and rejoice in. There must also be disciplines for those who wish only to mouth the word and not live the life. But other than those moral limitations, it is vital that the leaders stop imposing what they feel the community ought to believe and do. They should find out what God is doing in the group and then do what *they* are interested in. Overseers are to oversee. The role of the leader is not to do the job but to make sure the job gets done.

In many Christian groupings the leaders are over-worked; they're continually moaning at the people under their charge—but nothing ever changes. A slave society is what the leaders really want, where the decisions come from the top. There's little room for personal or corporate development inside the structure of the church/fellow-ship/community. Then there's rebellion in the camp, and a proliferation of para-church organizations for prayer, evangelism, inner-healing etc spring up, where people can develop their gifts and abilities. But all of that should be happening within the local church. We should be continually giving each other the freedom to develop our gifts and abilities in fellowship with others, working together in harness, to honour Christ and further the cause of the gospel of the kingdom.

There will always be people who want to do their own thing. People who are accountable to nobody and only referring to leaders when things go wrong. That's not at all what I'm talking about here. We don't want lone rangers making a platform for their own usefulness and ministry and then expecting the church to get behind it. I'm talking about giving each other the liberty to develop the abilities God has given us in our fellowship together, working and coping with all the tensions that come about in an active, gifted body of people.

The slave mentality restricts, damages, frustrates and

eventually kills off any real usefulness, and folk do nothing at all or almost only what's expected of them. It makes for a quiet life, but it doesn't make for the kingdom of God.

8. Failure to bring discipline

A submissive attitude often erases the need for strong judgements, either from ourselves or others. A submissive attitude to the Holy Spirit, the Scriptures and those around us will not ruin our self-esteem and do further damage to our bruised ego. In fact it will do quite the opposite.

Many people feel insignificant and therefore tend to be defensive and aggressive; they boast to cover up their insecurities. Their behaviour is often assertive, competitive and threatening, even though, because they have lived with it for so long, they are not aware of it. This of course is the opposite of submissive behaviour.

We cannot reach our full potential as members of the body of Christ unless we are willing to bend ourselves to the body of the believers we are a part of. If we are unwilling to do that, we should either check out our own attitude or move! It is hopeless working with a body of people who you secretly feel need to bend to you, with no change on your part. It will never happen anyway—unless you are a most gifted, extraordinary leader! Even so, it is not God's will for us to make such unreasonable demands on each other.

The church is filled with people who are trying to bend the body to their own whims and fancies. We must not abandon our critical faculties, and we must give each other the right to have reservations about what we are doing, but having done all of that, we must yield ourselves to our Christian community. Failure to do that will mean a stand-offish attitude, which works against the leaders, undermining authority and eventually being out of fellowship. Today there are thousands of people in churches throughout Britain who are out of fellowship but who are officially in 'the fellowship'. The failure to bring discipline in such situations does not only mean that we have some born-again, Spirit-filled believers in fellowship and some out; it also means that all sorts of people can eventually attach themselves to us, even those who don't know the Lord but are merely religious. All pretending to be 'in fellowship'.

I've already quoted Donald Grey-Barnhouse who said, 'It is our business to see that we do right. God will see to it that we come out right.' This is particularly true in the whole area of discipline, and that is why I have devoted an entire chapter to the issue (see chapter 11). However, it needs to be said here that the failure to bring discipline is another major reason why churches level off or collapse.

We must learn to be unafraid to receive and to exercise discipline in a loving, clean and honest way. Somebody once prayed, 'Lord, when we are wrong, make us willing to admit it and change. When we are right, make us easy to live with!' Such a prayer and attitude would do away with the ungodly fears that the word *discipline* conjures up. But without that attitude and without discipline, no local community could extend or display God's kingdom, for God is a God of judgement. While all the world will one day be judged, we Christians don't have to wait! We can receive his judgements now. God's plumbline of truth will come to us in many ways as we welcome it.

In conclusion

Where the King is ruling, there is his kingdom. I am sure that attention given to these eight areas will make for a healthy body of people.

Of course if all we do is get the concept but not the

substance, we shall be in trouble. If the King is going to be seen ruling, we must have the substance of his rulership and kingdom within us. If our own foundations are wonky, if our direction is lost and our judgements hopelessly inaccurate, we will not be able to extend these qualities to others. When Jesus said 'Peace' (Jn 20:19) he wasn't just uttering words, he gave them peace. He'd got it, therefore he could give it. We must face the fact that if we haven't got it, we must devote ourselves to the will and the word of God until we have got it; then we can give it—for his glory and for the blessing of others.

Chapter 10

A Kingdom Divided...

> Like a mighty tortoise moves the church of God;
> Brothers we are treading where we have always trod;
> We are all divided, not one body we,
> Very strong on doctrine, not much charity!

So goes the parody of the famous hymn, causing on the one hand a lot of laughter and, on the other, tears and heartache. Bad humour is of course an evasion of reality, while good humour is an acceptance of it. Judge for yourself which this is.

If there is one thing that is hampering the work of the Holy Spirit in Britain at the moment, it is the sin of sectarianism—party spirit, disunity and exclusive, or superior attitudes. Unless we get clear on the issue of 'what is unity?' the current blessing of God may cause multitudes to be personally fulfilled but without advancing God's kingdom.

The sin of division among God's people is paralysing the emerging army of believers called to follow Jesus, and it is the major reason why there has been a lack of power in our proclamation of the gospel. It is my firm belief that one of the reasons our local churches have a *'week* of unity' is because we do not want unity for the other fifty-one weeks of the year! With a few exceptions, most Christians make little attempt to relate on a day-to-day basis across the denominational barriers.

Different but the same

It is of course true that our levels of fellowship will be affected by differences of vision, theological perspective and practice. But fellowship is based on the fact that we have the same Father, not on whether we are charismatic, Calvinistic, traditional, conservative, or radical.

Recently I met with a group of clergy and house-group leaders who were somewhat suspicious of my presence in their city. It became clear that they were concerned that I would start 'yet another denomination'. After an hour of discussion, eventually I reasoned, 'If denominations are wrong, what are you doing to get out of them? And if they are not wrong, does it really matter whether we have one more, or a hundred more!' The logic, it seems, was either too profound or too stupid. Apparently we have enough denominations, and while leaders do not intend, desire or plan to dismantle their structures to further genuine unity, they certainly don't want any more structures! So we live in a no-man's-land where we don't want further division but where we have learned to live fairly happily with the divisions we have got.

Division and sectarianism

Recently I preached in a large Pentecostal church which was breaking away from traditional patterns. One of the first things the pastor felt had to be dealt with was the choir! They had dominated every service and, while he had an appreciation of the choir, he wanted them to be seen to be under the authority of the leadership and fulfilling their ministry by serving the eldership. So he told them quite clearly but kindly that they would not be needed at every service but could occasionally sit in the congregation and worship. This would, he added, give them more time for family commitments and other areas of fellowship, as they would not have to attend so many practices. On that issue alone over a hundred people walked out and went to another more traditional Pentecostal church where the choir was virtually the main feature of every service.

With the current proliferation of house fellowships it is becoming even easier to break fellowship over the tiniest issues. The breaking of fellowship usually does more damage to a local body of believers than the actual issue that causes the breakdown. While Paul was a seeker after the truth and, it seems, pursued the truth with all his heart, he was keen to acknowledge the grace of God wherever he went, whether it be in Jews or Gentiles. I'm sure he would have been glad to see God's grace in Calvinists, charismatics, conservative traditionalists, house-fellowship types, and all the other shades of theology and opinion not vitally essential to our fundamental unity.

What is vital, supremely significant, and so utterly necessary, is a real relationship with the Lord Jesus, based upon the revelation and confession that Jesus the Christ died, rose again and now lives in history and, wonder of wonders—in me! At the age of eleven I was brought to Christ with the verse, 'If you confess with your mouth Jesus as Lord, and believe in your heart that God raised Him from the dead, you shall be saved; for with the heart man believes, resulting in righteousness, and with the mouth he confesses, resulting in salvation. For the Scripture says, whoever believes in Him will not be disappointed' (Rom 10:9–11). It is the gospel that unites and only a denial of that gospel must separate us.

The elusive dream

In the early seventies there was a fresh impetus, initiated by the Holy Spirit, to bring God's people together. Men of varying theological persuasions and church backgrounds experienced the Holy Spirit in a vital way.

The fatherhood of God over all those who had a relationship with the Lord Jesus began to unite these believers. But soon the air of excitement and euphoria gave way to heartbreak and disappointment. One man after another either became impatient or began to build groups of people around his particular theological persuasion, church structure, apostolic authority and concepts of leadership. Or else they simply faded away into safe areas where they would never be challenged or hurt.

Over and over again it seems that we are willing to forsake valuable relationships, using as an excuse the desire to 'get the job done'. Rather than simply widen our circle of friendships, which should happen in the course of life, we actually drop past relationships, sometimes of several years standing. We need to appreciate that the job *is* relationships. When all is said and done, that is all we are going to have left. Everything is to be done through relationships, and it is the gospel that gives us those relationships.

It is of course possible to make relationships a standard, or a place where false security can be found. But we need to understand that God himself is giving us relationships with each other for *his* purposes, not simply our own.

We should be building relationships with believers in our localities, and elsewhere, acknowledging our differences while extending grace to each other in areas of behaviour and theology. Instead, new national networks are springing up, only adding to the already established network of State, Free, Evangelical and Pentecostal churches. These are united not in the truth of salvation through Christ alone but of salvation plus doctrine, method, personalities, or use of Scripture. It is not that these things are unimportant, but they must never be allowed to destroy the relationships that God has created through the gospel. Even those who bang the drum loudest for the cause of the gospel 'and only the gospel', on close inspection will be found to have written off vast sections of the body of Christ—written off not because such groups do not believe in the supreme importance of the gospel, but because of their charismatic emphasis, or dancing and drama in meetings, or non-sabbath observance, or whatever.

The continual tendency to surround ourselves with a group of clones or proselytes has got to be changed. We must be a radical and prophetic voice on the one hand, while endeavouring to build relationships with *all* believers on the other. Unfortunately, it tends to be one or the other. Either you are a prophetic voice building relationships with nobody, or you seek to build relationships everywhere until the voice has been lost amidst the religious paraphernalia of twentieth-century churchianity.

The qualities which exist within the Godhead can characterize God's people. Mercy, love, forgiveness, grace, judgement and truth can saturate each of us. If the life of Christ is given free reign, we shall be amazed at what will happen in our locality!

A *critique of denominationalism*

Denominationalism is sin! It is heresy! There is no way round it. Heresy does not necessarily mean what is normally implied today. If someone is branded a heretic it is generally thought that that person has erred from truth, that he is now teaching unbiblical principles. History is full of people who have been burned at the stake, drowned, or lashed for departing from some so-called truth or another. But this is not what the word *heresy* meant to the early church.

It is not only error that divides—many use the truth to turn brother against brother. So heresy is an attitude of heart, bent on having its own way. Sometimes separation is necessary, as with Abraham and Lot, but always the desire is for the good of God's people. The Holy Spirit is able to fellowship with us and work with us despite our differences!

But how different it is when we come to work with one another. The Bible says that if men have repented of their sin, sought to make restitution for past wrongs, and are seeking to devote themselves to Jesus, we must receive them and where possible work with them. God enjoys their friendship and fellowship and accepts them irrespective of their theological positions. We must do the same.

I enjoy good fellowship and often a lot of laughs, as well as prayer, with Anglican priests, Calvinistic preachers, Roman Catholic fathers and house-church leaders of many types. In no way do I feel I have to justify my position or personally attack them for theirs. I may feel that a dog-collar looks lunatic, that papal authority is a nonsense, or that infant baptism as stated in the Anglican prayer-book is erroneous, but these differences need not hinder fellowship. To me, religious buildings, altars and restrictive forms of worship are things I left behind years ago, but I can still relate to those who continue to believe in them. God is not calling us to compromise over issues we feel we have had to make a stand over. And that is true of other people, as they look at me in what I am doing. We can share in honesty without writing one another off. We do not need doctrinal or behavioural conformity to love one another. It is often regarded as being unloving to disagree with one another, whereas in fact it may be the most loving thing to do. Our difficulty is that we feel unable to express our differences while still maintaining a depth of fellowship. So we either push things down and pretend such differences do not exist, or bombard each other from a safe distance.

Guilt by association

If Jesus is to be our example, the 'guilt by association' argument is blown to smithereens. It was the religious people who criticized him for eating and drinking with sinners. But he also had a number of men among his close friendships and acquaintances who were clearly identified with religious systems. Some like Zacchaeus were corrupt and petty, while others, in the Lord's own words, would rather strain out a gnat and swallow a camel (Mt 23:24) than deal with the real issues of life. In that environment creatures often found their way into foods, and it was a common sight to see the folk straining them out. So Jesus was saying that these people enjoyed majoring on tenth-rate issues while evading God's first-rate ones. But Jesus knew that if he was looking to start with a like-minded group of men to fellowship with, he would be on his own!

The problem with many leaders is that because of an inability to relate to people in reality, they can only think in terms of their denomination relating to another denomination. Therefore a Calvinistic denomination or a Calvinistic non-denominational denomination (which is even worse) refuses to relate to the Roman Catholic denomination. But we cannot relate to a denomination. It is a piece of paper. We can only relate to *people*.

I do not understand why many people are in groups and organizations, and maybe others cannot understand why I am doing what I am doing. But to relate to me does not mean you have got to relate to the whole of the house-church movement. To share a platform with David Watson does not mean I have to agree with the Anglican prayerbook, any more than he will agree with everything in this book. If Pawson, Muggeridge, Suenens, Wallis, Coates and Delve shared a platform together, it would not mean that they had all been smitten by an attack of total theological agreement!

In an attempt to create security, many churches now have statements of faith which members are asked to sign. Of course there is a world of difference between mentally agreeing to a list of articles and having those truths grip the heart of the signatory. On one statement of faith it is declared that all those who have rejected the gospel go to hell. Personally, I doubt whether the average evangelical believer is actually gripped with that fact (despite his signature). Loads of people live and work among these believers. But despite such signed declarations most have never been pressed to receive Christ. So who is believing what?

We are back to the old answer to every spiritual ill. If you can't make the people spiritual, just make it look as though they are spiritual, equipping believers with theological creeds, statements of faith, plus an agreed statement of opinion on about almost everything. Such statements of faith, in my opinion, are generally an utter waste of time and only serve to create further division. A man will believe what he believes. What he believes is totally dependent on how much he is willing to allow Jesus, who is the truth, to rule over his life and affairs. How much he is willing to receive the Scriptures and absorb them into his being. Membership of the church takes place the moment he is born of God and begins to live out of a life that honours Jesus. It is somewhat peculiar that those who believe in the Bible the most fervently, create an unbiblical 'membership' which they believe is based upon a biblical foundation!

Competition or co-operation?

The result of this disunity is either competition or total disregard at all levels. Churches are valued on the size of their buildings and congregations, whether there is a choir, a Sunday school, how much Bible teaching there is, and so on.

The spirit of co-operation, other than at the most superficial levels, in most localities is virtually non-existent. The odd crisis, church scandal, or evangelistic campaign may briefly bring believers together. But when everything's died down, we scurry back to our safe areas, at best competing with other churches or disregarding them altogether. Unless of course they take one of our members! Then a flurry of activity begins which is out of all proportion to the problem. We must allow folk to settle where they will flourish best. People have left our group in Cobham and have been sent to the local C of E with our blessing—and vice versa.

On to maturity

God requires that those in any measure of responsibility do everything possible to create harmony, understanding and unity among all who have found Jesus as their Saviour and Lord. Leaders within families, youth fellowships, cell groups, local congregations, music groups, para-church organizations, are all to adopt the same attitude.

To preach the gospel while maintaining divisions is to

think we can achieve good by resorting to evil methods. The church teems with reliable, inoffensive, well-intentioned people who believe passionately that the church should be one, while at the same time maintaining existing divisions to the *n*th degree. We have been left to our fantasies for too long. Wake up, Zion!

I am not talking about ecumenism. We can have no faith whatever in the current attempts to merge denominations. Can we expect anything other than a bigger hotch-potch than we have already? It may be the religious thing to do, quoting John 17 and nodding in approval, closing down half-empty buildings and putting as many people as possible under one roof. But that is not the church! The church has not got so much to do with meetings as it has to do with life. If people in those denominations are not already relating in life, then putting them together in one building will do nothing to advance the kingdom and create the sort of unity that the gospel makes possible.

In Britain at the time of writing, the denomination that is losing more people and experiencing minimal church growth in terms of converts is the result of two major denominations 'uniting'. History has proven that the way to multiplication is by organic division, not organizational unity.

Holy anger

As a de-programmed evangelical I am beginning to understand how much of our local church life grieves the Lord and, I fear, will soon rouse his anger. Aristotle once declared, 'Anyone can become angry, that's easy; but to be angry with the right person to the right degree, at the right time, for the right purpose and in the right way, that is not easy.' But God's anger is perfect, not only in quality but in timing. How long will the Lord put up with our petty divisions, defensive attitudes, and allow the carnal, unspiritual, fearful and prejudiced to motivate decisions? When will men and women make a stand for righteousness?

Fantasy or fact?

Being a keen observer of church life, I have observed the following:

1. Official truth is not necessarily the truth

The feelings of 'the people' are not always reflected by the leadership. Russia is a classic illustration. Less than one in ten are members of the Communist Party!

Recently I lunched with a well-known figure in the evangelical church who confessed he was somewhat surprised how much he enjoyed friendship with various people in the Cobham community. 'Officially', due to things he had heard about us, he adopted a suspicious and careful stance based on rumour and hearsay. In reality, he got on so well he even considered moving to Cobham! That gave him a good dose of George Orwell's 'double-think'!

It is somewhat different with many ministers, clergy, house-group leaders and public figures who have a genuine desire for unity but are hampered by the groups of people they are responsible for. Here the 'official truth' of the leader is disregarded as his whim or fancy rather than the burden of the Spirit.

Coming from a sectarian Brethren background, I smile at the complete turnaround that I have experienced in the last few years. For, while 'officially' we are outside the fold of the Roman Catholic Church and are 'separated brethren', I am now enjoying genuine fellowship with many Roman Catholics and clergy. On the other hand, Pentecostal denominations (which one might have imagined would be delighted about the charismatic movement) have more problems with what I am doing, saying and writing than some of the more historic churches!

2. *Definitive lines do not create perfection*

Most groupings have unwritten lists of speakers and organizations who are either 'in' or 'out'. C. Northcote Parkinson stated in one of his famous laws that definitive lines and perfection of layout are achieved only by institutions on the verge of collapse. And so it was that the Vatican completed the structure of St Peter's just as the Protestant Reformation broke out!

It is still sadly true that if you offer a blurred and a clear picture of things, the vast majority will always go for the clear, irrespective of how true it is. We dislike ambiguity, and we must face the fact that people have a tendency to choose groups with clear, albeit false assumptions and promises. Remembering the mystery that there is in life and in the gospel itself, we would do well to ponder this.

At present, the greatest vitality and growth among God's people is outside institutional Christianity. But once principles have been formulated, the unclear has been made clear, the lost has been found, clear pictures emerge as to what is right and wrong, who is 'in' and 'out', then the definitive suffocates the life. I well remember how at school we had to write a definitive essay on the inner workings of a frog. Pinned out on a wooden board, the frog was duly cut up and I wrote an excellent essay as a result of this experiment. But the frog died!

Happy are those who are willing to live with the mystery, with blurred edges. Happy are those who have not got all the ends tied together, who are still seeking after a King and his kingdom even though they have found the King and are a part of that kingdom. Happy are those whose faith is in God and not in definitives. Happy are those who desire to relate wherever there is fellowship based upon the mutual sharing of life in Christ.

3. *We must lose some things to gain others*

As we progress from youth to maturity, it is inevitable that we lose and gain certain things. I have noticed that infants have a habit of wanting what they have not got while retaining what they have in their hand! But sometimes we must lay aside past blessing, and lay hold of the 'new thing' that God is doing. This can be the same in family relationships. Families, for one reason or another, have feuds, people separate on principle, but generations of family feuds become meaningless and irrelevant. A 'new thing' happens and people find they like each other, or have a need to relate together, despite ancestral feuding.

In the past, where two feuding families wanted to come together, the daughter from one family was chosen for marriage with a son of the other family. But in the best novels, the lady and gentleman in question fall in love! As a result, a whole new group of people, indeed another family, are included into the circle of the first family.

We must be unafraid of committing our love to people of different persuasions. We must stop thinking about the consequences and the ramifications of doing what is obvious and natural to bring honour and glory to God. The result is then almost bound to be an inclusion of other families into our own circle, or vice versa.

I have already touched on the new groups that are currently emerging. Once they are fairly sure of their identity, they then have something to give to the rest of the redeemed community, as well as those outside the kingdom. But many of the more established groups need to come to a place where they are willing to lose their present identity in order to be absorbed into something much better.

4. *Emotional pressure must give way to leadership*

Whether it be the unity of a family, cell group or congregation, it is probably fair to say that too much time is spent dashing around our area of responsibility, placating and reassuring where we should in fact be giving clear leadership. People can follow leadership, but where there is no leadership everybody becomes functionally equal. Everyone's opinions matter. Many leaders end up spending most of their time putting out bush fires that are a direct result of their own lack of clear direction.

Most of our activity will fail to create unity unless we are really leading the way. One church I know of had a bad case of 'fellowshipitis'. So they doubled the meetings to talk about the situation! Another church, feeling intimidated by the growth of nearby fellowships, pressurized their folk to go on a door-to-door visitation programme. It turned out to be an almost total waste of time. So they came up with an answer: to double their efforts in the coming months! The competitive spirit increased and they became motivated by the urgent and not the important.

The urgent has to do with hand-to-mouth situations; the important with where we'll be as a community in ten or twenty years' time. We need to experience the novelty of being different, getting out of religious thinking. To do this we will need to give clear leadership in our spheres of responsibility.

Church leadership involves taking initiative, clarifying situations, elaborating where there is misunderstanding, drawing on resources and information, encouraging the feeble and relieving unnecessary conflicts. It involves drawing people out from self-centredness to be continually serving God. It demands that we encourage people away from secrecy to the sharing of their lives, giving them a sense of moral responsibility both for themselves and others.

Emotional support is of course at times necessary, but many of us in responsibility spend far too much time giving it rather than leading. Instead of dealing with people's fears we often feed them because we are fearful ourselves. Most of the fears people have have been implanted by other people. So let leaders lead, followers follow, and let's be done with having continually to respond to coercive pressure.

Proclaiming in reality

The greatest proclamation of the gospel will be the oneness of God's people. Where else on earth can we expect to see men of every cultural background, theological persuasion and colour living in harmony? Learning to live with their differences and resolve their problems? Willing to learn from each other rather than defending their own preconceived positions? In God's kingdom it is a crime to walk alone, and the sight of old and young, black and white, poor and wealthy, sharing life together will say more than any preacher can say.

'Any kingdom divided against itself is laid waste,' said our King (Mt 12:15). How seriously do we take him? We are divided organizationally. We are divided by outmoded traditions which have already proved inadequate, and by new ones that smack of superiority and are therefore doomed as well. We are divided by the buildings we meet in. We are divided by continually drawing upon circles of like-minded speakers. We are divided by continually listening to rumours about one another, feeding prejudice and fear. We are divided by our interpretations of important parts of Scripture. We are divided by what we think constitutes leadership. We are divided by whether or not we believe in the gifts of the Spirit, particularly tongues and prophecy! Divided! Divided! Divided! Yes, we are divided! Where are the men and women who will break out of divisive attitudes, fearful spirits and restricting structures, and live out the high-priestly prayer of Jesus, 'that they may be one' (Jn 17:11)? Let's take the first step now! Let's begin by believing that maybe *someone* outside our own circle might have something of value to say—we could be in for a surprise!

Unity in Christ!

So we return again to my oft-repeated theme throughout this book, that fellowship with Christ and one another is not found in religious ways of believing or doing things. It is found in a shared experience of Christ who from a moral point of view has left us in no doubt as to how we are to live. Jesus accepted and quoted the Scriptures, so we should have no problem with that one. 'My sheep hear my voice and I know them and they follow me' (Jn 10:27). Unity is found in knowing Christ and in being found and known by Christ. Unity will never come by knowing a lot about Christ. The incredible and marvellous thing about the Christian faith is this: Jesus the author and founder of our faith is alive! He is everywhere and at work all over the world, but he is specifically seen among his people, to demonstrate the reality of what the whole world is looking for. Peace, unity and love.

This increasing knowledge of Christ by his people does not normally take place in isolation. Isolation becomes the fertile sowing ground for the enemy. Writing to believers in Ephesus, Paul told them that he was praying that they 'being rooted and grounded in love, may be able to comprehend *with all the saints* what is the breadth and length and height and depth, and to know the love of Christ which surpasses knowledge' (Eph 3:17–19, italics mine). Together, with all true believers, we can stand knowing that 'only the gospel can do this'. Divided we may not actually fall—just hinder, frustrate and grieve the Holy Spirit! We may merely fade away, off the face of the earth, confronted with other spreading religions, powerful political parties, strong ideas whose time has come. But together! Together walking in the morality of Christ, loving one another as he loves us, despite our deficiencies and cultural differences, his government can and will be extended.

Not all division is bad. Obviously we need to be divided from the carnal, the worldly, those who will not acknowledge Jesus Christ as Saviour and Lord—even if they put on a show of religion. Yes we need to be divided from all of that, and yet we are to understand that we are also the very instruments of reconciliation and salvation to those very people. Of course we are not to be divided from others who love the Lord Jesus, who honour holy writings inspired by the Holy Spirit and yet do things differently. We are to dialogue and fellowship together wherever possible, with a view to understanding and learning. We may need, as I have done on occasions, to speak out against legalism, empire building, settling spirits, and the sort of divisiveness which is not based upon God's word. We must be ready to receive that kind of ministry when it comes from men who we sense care for us. There must be a willingness to give and receive correction. But behind it all must be an overwhelming desire to fellowship, share life and be involved with each other.

We are one! We simply need to find ways of expressing our unity. We must put aside all that divides us that is not in accordance with God's holy will, so that the unity and oneness can be something more than a sentimental, well-meaning exercise. Let our unity contain teeth, guts, substance and reality! And, for God's sake, let's start loving now!

Chapter 11

Kingdom Judgement—A Change of Attitude

They must have been the thickest bifocals in the world, and I wasn't sure whether he was looking at me or not! With one hand he gave me the hymn book and with the other...? Well, it was so limp I didn't know whether to shake it, nurse it, hit it or pray for it! He also had a serious speech impediment, so I wasn't sure whether my welcome to the church was in Swahili or angelic tongues!

Later I discovered that the entire church was embarrassed by Stanley, who had been greeting folk at the door for well over twenty years. It was a frequent subject of discussion but nobody wanted to say anything to him for fear of offending him. They all knew that he was the least suited man for the job, but they all knew in confidence! The only one who didn't know was Stanley. They had swept their embarrassment and annoyance under the carpet. Soon the protrusions would wear thin and all would be exposed.

Multiply this situation over and over again, and there we have the reason for so much behind-the-scenes wrangling and church politics. No judgement. No final conclusions. Nothing is ever brought to a head. Diplomacy and fear rule.

The fear of offending people has allowed a situation to emerge where those with large or luxurious homes give hospitality, despite serious marital problems. Where boring communicators with nothing to say have become platform and pulpit preachers. Where thrifty bank managers have been appointed as treasurers. (Usually a mistake—ask any travelling speaker or musician!) Where adults who don't get on with other adults give themselves to children's work instead. In most churches such situations are rarely faced with the truth.

The line of least resistance

The temple, I am told, was built on the threshing floor of Ornan. It was a place of judgement, where wheat was divided from chaff. All worship, sacrifice, prayer and offerings were made in the light of judgement. What is and what is not acceptable to God his judgements make crystal clear. The Lord builds relationships with us on the basis of his judgements and our response to them. Jesus' first mention of the church was in connection with judgement (Mt 18:15–17). Not—as one would suppose— evangelism, prayer, fasting, doctrine, or the gifts of the Spirit.

Judgement in relationships

In effect Jesus said, 'John, if you have a problem with Andrew, go and see him. Not to score a point or even to correct him. Go to win him. Winning your brother is more important than being right. Of course if he will not even listen to you, you must take a couple of unbiased friends to witness the situation—to watch your attitude as well as his. It could be that *he* is being unreasonable or that *you* are gunning for him! You need friends to witness such attitudes. If he still refuses to listen to any of you then you must tell that section of God's people he relates to, and if he won't listen to them you treat him as an outsider. If people will not submit to the family, they cannot be in the family.'

I can imagine John reacting, 'But Lord, it is such a silly issue, why do we need to do all this?' And I'm sure that the Lord would have told him that the 'silly issue' was no longer the issue. Any brother unwilling to hear his brothers is out of fellowship. He is a law unto himself and must be treated as such. I can see John interrupting again. 'But Lord, if we did this as you ask, we'd be doing it all the time—we'd never get anything done!' 'Not so,' I think our Lord would have replied, since he knew that if people do not talk out their problems and judgement is never brought, they remain divided for years, putting up a façade of pretence.

Sitting on committees, taking on responsibilities, having Bible studies, or even the sharing of bread and wine, do not necessarily constitute fellowship. John, Jesus' best friend, made it abundantly clear that we can only have true fellowship when we 'walk in the light' (1 Jn 1:7). If we will not do that, we are guilty of breaking fellowship, and sooner or later this must be brought to judgement.

The curse of doublemindedness

What happens if we fail to walk in the light? How important is it? George Orwell in his book *1984* wrote, 'Double-think means the ability of holding two contradictory beliefs in one's mind simultaneously and accepting them both.' In practice it goes something like this: John is a 'dear brother' in public, but in private is an 'absolute pain'. Or

Stanley as we've referred to is 'fulfilling a wonderful function in the church, he's such a faithful brother, he's been doing it for years'. But *actually* everybody feels, 'It's such an embarrassment having him at the door, I'd never bring anybody to this church!' People who fail to bring judgement are not only unfaithful but are doublethinkers. Doublethinkers say different things in different situations. A doubleminded man is unstable in all his ways (Jas 1:8). A doubleminded person has multitudes of opinions but cannot have any convictions. It is almost impossible to build relationships with people like this, as on almost every issue they keep changing position!

We need to be praying regularly, 'Lord, I accept your judgements, I choose to receive them and make them.' It is no good waiting until we get cornered, until group pressure piles up on us. God wants us to act, not react. We must choose to follow the right course from the beginning as things rarely get better. Time does not heal in these situations; rather it is because we leave it to time that time determines the outcome of such situations. And it's seldom what we want. It's no good sweeping things under the carpet saying, 'It doesn't matter.' As we have seen, life will become a little bumpy after a while!

Judgement at home—personal repentance

It is of course impossible to build into the community around us what we have failed to build into our own families. The reason people take so little notice of what Christians recommend is the disorderly state of our families. We may make progress by our gift and ability, or our pleasant personality, but we're often keen to lay things on others while our own families are escaping judgement left, right and centre. If we cannot bring judgement at home we will never successfully bring it elsewhere. And even if we do, there will be a lack of respect because they know our home situation.

On one occasion Anona and I had a problem. Numerous discussions (a rather pleasant way of putting it!) had brought deadlock. We invited a close friend to intervene and bring judgement. He listened to both sides of the story. 'Anona, you need to change your attitude. You must not be so selfish; be more sensitive and considerate towards Gerald,' he said. I leaned back on my garden chair breathing in the fresh morning air and feeling things were not working out so bad after all! 'And as for you,' he continued, turning on me, 'your attitude is appalling. Can't you see the pressure you are putting on Anona?' I was so flabbergasted I nearly fell off my chair—backwards! Apart from Anona he was my best friend. It was not an easy situation; perhaps I ought to find another close friend! But I chose to submit to his judgements. Of course there is no point asking people to bring judgement to situations if we have no intention of submitting to them. It is very easy to give others what we would not receive ourselves, but as we have seen, those exercising authority must be seen to be under authority.

Fatherly judgement

Two local boys used to come and play with my eldest son. One respected the family, my leadership and the home. He was willing to submit to the running order of the household. He was therefore treated as a part of our family. But then there was the other lad! He had no respect for me, Anona or our property. However, we put up with him! Our three boys occasionally played with him, frequently got into trouble with him, and at times they formed a strong alliance. But one thing they would never do was treat him as part of the family. The reason was obvious. He wasn't rightly related to their father! What was more obvious was that Anona and I didn't treat him as a part of the family either—for the same reason.

One reason why we fear judgement is that we relate the very word to courtroom drama. A cold, calculated process, without love and affection. Judgement we assume only exists to make sure that the law is upheld. However, within the context of friendship, love and care, judgement becomes a major factor in our security.

Family relationships must be developed. We must know who our spiritual fathers are. Where father-figures are respected, judgement on issues large and small can be brought with affection, kindness and truth. Judgement should be a normal, regular and welcome part of our lives together. Not a one-off crisis that is hopefully never faced again. We need to allow ourselves to be fathered, encouraged and corrected, so that we can do the same to others. It is simply not enough to be taught only from the front of a meeting.

It is vital that we honour those who have cared for us by blessing and encouraging them, and letting them know that their words, attitudes and judgements matter. Fathering and judgement go hand in hand. If we will allow ourselves to be fathered with all the judgements that come with such a relationship, we will become fit fathers in the house of God ourselves. On one occasion Paul longed for fathers to emerge among God's people. He told them they had many teachers, people willing to tell them what to do, but not many fathers willing to be responsible for the practical outworking (1 Cor 4:15).

Corporate judgement

Judgement is not the exclusive task of pastors, fathers or house-group leaders. Too often it falls solely on their shoulders. The daunting prospect of facing individuals and at times the whole church, invariably alone, is enough to keep them awake at night and weaken their hearts by day!

During the exodus of the Jews, we read that Jethro advised Moses to delegate his authority. It was vital that the people were taught to resolve their own disputes, not simply to get the leaders to sort them out for them. Today leaders must teach people how to manage their own affairs, or they will be in danger of suffering nervous breakdowns. What's more, the people will never mature and grow up. Leaders are supposed to oversee other people working out their own salvation.

One young man in our fellowship received judgement and confessed before us that resentment and bitterness had built up in his life over a period of years. He had been spoken to just once about this issue by his 'spiritual father'. His problem revolved around the way God was using other folk in our community who had been with us as long as he had. He submitted to the words of correction and felt the only way to put things right was through a public apology. He asked for the church's forgiveness and the channels of fellowship between him and those he resented were wonderfully reopened.

Stephen, on the other hand, reluctantly confessed to certain serious misdemeanours in his life after he had been found out! It was not a leadership issue, but a moral one. A number of his friends and acquaintances were called together to hear his confession. The brothers placed restrictions and constraints on him which also included regular times of fellowship, discussion and prayer until trust re-emerged. It was not felt necessary to tell the whole church, simply those who were related to him. In this kind of situation there must never be a cover-up. Invariably the facts come out. Without judgement people eventually assume things that have got nothing to do with what happened, thus creating suspicion, fear and doubt.

Open judgement

It is important that serious issues are not kept secret. News leaks out and rumours become rife with mistrust growing all round. Without trust progress is impossible. I want people to trust me on the basis of what they know about me, not on the basis of what they don't know about me. There is far too much secrecy, innuendo, suggestive comment and shadiness in people's talk. Wherever it's appropriate we need to be open, honest and clean.

One day the whole world will be judged. It will then be too late for those involved. But, as we have already noted, God's people do not have to wait to be judged. As we receive God's judgements we will be better equipped to make sound judgements ourselves. Paul tells us that one day we will even judge angels (1 Cor 6:3). So we need to choose to bring loving and clear judgement to situations where we are required to do so.

Facing the issues of judgement may not be the smartest way to keep a well-integrated, unruffled personality. We may feel all over the place emotionally as we go through the fire. But God asks us to be morally consistent, not emotionally consistent. If we endeavour to be emotionally consistent, it will lead to all sorts of untruthfulness and pretence. 'Do you think I ought to do so and so?' asks a friend. 'Oh yes!' we say, assuming that is what our friend wants to hear. We maintain our emotional level of ease but are grossly unfaithful. A few heartaches later they come and share the crisis that has resulted from taking the course we approved of. Yet again we are faced with being either emotionally or morally consistent. If we seek to be morally consistent it may not make for the ingredients of emotional consistency, but it will make us better people and, more to the point, bring Christ the highest accolade possible.

God's kingdom is not to be shot through with shoddy attitudes and hidden but growing hurts. It is a kingdom of wonderful judgement. 'The judgements of the Lord are true' (Ps 19:9). And so it should be among us all!

Repentance—the key

Not every conflict demands repentance. Problems are there to be overcome. But it is sin that requires repentance. We must face the fact that in the course of life there will always be misunderstandings, a measure of insensitivity, many things which are not plain and simple. They are an expression of our immature personalities and energies.

However, when the Holy Spirit points out sin, repentance and a change of attitude must follow if we are to continue in fellowship with the Lord. A preacher was once arguing with the Lord, when he felt he heard the Lord say, 'Bob, you and I are incompatible—and I don't change!' Over issues of sin there is only one party that needs to change—and that's us!

Repentance turns us from sin, selfishness and individualism. It releases us from bondage to self, to what others think, and to demons. Repentance turns us from all that binds and oppresses us. It renders inoperative all the false gods we may have worshipped and all the powers that seek to manipulate and control us. It deals with our past, our destinies as well as our day-to-day living.

The new birth, the fullness of the Spirit and the corporate, shared life are not a self-improvement course or a set of guidelines for happy living, though they may accomplish both. They have to do with being a prophetic statement to those around us. The people of God around us have fallen into disobedience, lukewarmness and idolatry. God is looking for a people no longer dominated by its own needs, but rather one that wants to find and do his will.

Things or people

Many Christians are materialistically orientated, with little daily experience of the Spirit of God. Irrespective of what Christ demands, most believers are individualists with no experience of shared life or community. If that was not the case we would no longer be motivated to accumulate wildly and plan and scheme for this, that and the other. If we were God-centred we would love one another! We would treat each other as if we were flesh and blood. We would share what we have with one another. Repentance would be a natural part of our lives. The judgement of God must be invited—concerning our attitude to things, money and the accumulation of the stuff of this world. With all of their beauty, offers of pleasure and comfort, they do not come anywhere near the fulfilment of being in Christ and being in fellowship with others. We can thank God for material blessings, but they are a bonus, not a right.

The judgements of God are coming to churches where self-fulfilment and individual promotion have become idols and goals. It is not surprising that our self-centred age has produced self-centred Christianity—including a self-centred charismatic Christianity. Young converts would be forgiven for coming to the conclusion that Jesus wants to help us succeed in this present order of things rather than face that order with a new order—the kingdom, the government of God. A well-integrated, successful, knowing-how-to-cope-in-every-situation-type individual is not the end of the Spirit-filled life. No, the end is brothers dwelling together in unity (see Ps 133:1).

While it is true that the gospel brings Jesus into our lives, it also brings us into his. The issue is not, how can Jesus fulfil our lives, though he will do that, but how can we fulfil his? This preoccupation with self must be eradicated. It has bred an attitude that says, 'If God is meeting our need here and now, that is all we are concerned about.' If things do not go right, we will seek his face to know his mind and will. But if things are going well through the accumulation of goods, comfortable bank accounts, and if we have overcome the major, overt sins of life, we somehow feel there's not much left to repent. Maybe the whole way we live needs to be judged!

Judgement and a new order

The bizarre situation we are faced with in Britain is that we have loads of 'saved' and 'baptized in the Spirit' individuals who fit very comfortably into the form and politics of this world, who are putting off the new order until some future date. Nevertheless a growing number of people are beginning to welcome the judgements of God into their lives and lifestyles. Having been converted to Christ, filled with the Spirit, or having found fellowship with others, they are now rightly asking, 'What is it all for?' We have answered the questions of 'how to' very well in this technological age. How to put a man on the moon, put a computer the size of a typewriter into ordinary homes, travel faster than the speed of sound, put moving pictures into every living room. But now people are asking, 'What's it all for?' And not before time.

The older generation of Christians are going to have to wrestle with this question. Just as many of them have moved out of a worldly, liberal or pharisaical stance, so many young people of our generation are going to move on from where the older ones have brought them.

God-given security

Once we become secure in the love, care and judgements of others, the need to be continually judging ourselves will cease. Once we lay down our defences and continually choose to hear the Holy Spirit and those around us, we will be able to use those judgements in ease.

'He who is afraid to ask questions, is afraid to show he still has need to learn,' goes the old Chinese proverb. Once we lose the ability to learn we cease to grow. The judgements of God will cause us to mature and grow, making us a viable force and voice in the world.

Chapter 12

My Mediocre Recommendations...

In the light of my observations, my mediocre recommendations for those who claim to be God's people in the
eighties are as follows. Sell all church buildings and use
the money to help the unemployed. Alternatively use
them for local community needs. Strip all clergy and
denominational leaders of ecclesiastical status and let
those with God's gifts get on and do what they have to do.
Close all religious academic training centres and Bible
schools and use the property to house the homeless.
Separate church and state where agnostics and atheists
influence the running of the so-called church. Arrange for
all 'full-time' Christian leaders to take a job every few
years to stay in touch with their culture and non-religious
people. Close all denominational headquarters overnight.
Abolish service/meeting oriented churches, to give way to
those built around friendships and commitment to one
another and to the Scripture.

The only exceptions to the above would be buildings of
historic and architectural value which should be supported
and owned by the National Trust and opened to the
public.

A blast for the past

The maintaining of musty, outdated, shabby church buildings should give way to the use of homes and the comparatively inexpensive hiring of halls and theatres. The dressing up of clergy in those ridiculous outfits should be abandoned. (Is there anything more lunatic than watching high-ranking ecclesiastical figures performing in tea-cosy headgear and gaiters?) Normal men and women in normal dress should go about the normal business of leading the church and bringing people to Christ. While there is some value in academic study, much of it bears little relevance to local fellowship life. It often creates armchair critics who know nothing about living life but a lot about the untried theory of it. I fancy Jesus and his disciples would never have passed the entrance exam, let alone the finals, in most Bible colleges!

The absurd marriage of church and state can only be likened to the vegetarian society being ultimately accountable to the Cattle Breeder's Association! To even imagine that every reigning monarch, prime minister and their political and religious advisers know the heart and mind of God when making top ecclesiastical appointments is laughable.

Some men have gone into 'the ministry' simply because they couldn't cope with their culture or perhaps the world of business. The church was a way of escape. Many church leaders would do well to be exposed to the realities of life found in a regular job. Much of what they have to say would then take on a different tone. Isolated from the real world we tend to preach one thing and live another.

One charismatic Anglican minister walked out of a meeting where several thousand were sharing bread and wine. His problem was simply that it wasn't done in the 'proper way'. In the light of the fact that he is required by law to give out bread and wine to anyone who is confirmed, irrespective of whether they are born again and know or love the Lord Jesus, I find it a somewhat bizarre situation. Denominational leaders who preach unity while building sectarianism are party to hypocrisy at its worst.

At a large meeting where a number of Spirit-filled Roman Catholics were present it was made quite clear to us that, if there was to be any form of communion or breaking of bread, the bishops should put a stop to it or forbid their people from attending. Again we see ecclesiastical institutionalism choking on the truth. The truth that there is only one church and the Spirit himself is bringing unity, is more than ecclesiastical barrels (hardly wineskins!) can cope with.

As it was in the beginning ...

Culturally most churches assume a somewhat static view of the future. If they imagine the future at all, they are planning on the basis that it will be made up of more of the present! Despite the growing gap between the cultures and traditions of churchianity and the rest of the nation, the church does not believe that such a gap exists. Nor would it close the gap if that meant changing the things I've mentioned.

However, far from fearing the world with its false values, high fashions, fast foods and drinks, its plethora of entertainments and pleasures, we should be using and at times even enjoying these things, not only to identify ourself with our culture, but also to share our faith. It is vital that we are not continually having to catch up with what's going on; rather we should be developing the ability to anticipate trends and learn to live fearlessly within our changing culture, without being dominated by it.

At wedding receptions, for example, most Christians

huddle at one end, drinking orange juice while those of 'the world' enjoy themselves with wine or Martini! 'What would they think of us?' is the defensive cry. Well, they would think exactly the same of you as they would of Jesus! He not only drank wine, he changed water into wine at a wedding reception! In fact he was called a wine-bibber, which is the nearest thing to a drunkard you could get! And when it is dancing time at receptions, what do we hear? 'It's time we left now dear,' apologizes Mr Christian. 'We must get back to our babysitter!' Christians just don't seem to know how to enjoy themselves and walk with God at the same time.

And on the issue of leadership it is so easy to lose touch with what is happening in the cultural/business/social world. The very men who are meant to be relating the gospel to our culture are the ones who have led us away from it!

Religious parrots

It has been said that the church is full of feather-bellied, hard-beaked and tiny-headed parrots. If someone says colour television is worldly, up goes the chorus 'Colour television is worldly'. When Christians eventually purchase colour television, for news and documentaries only of course, there is a change in our theology. There is nothing like a dose of experience to change one's theology! Meanwhile, as I write, video is still 'wildly extravagant and worldly'. Probably when you read this the theology will have been adapted again.

There is still a hidden, almost unconfessed fear that if believers are bang up-to-date culturally, with entertainment, dress, foods and leisure, they are probably not really walking with the Lord; they are immature and egoistic, or at best attention-seeking. So we dress in the fashions of ten or even twenty years ago, still maintaining a sort of spirituality by only having black-and-white television, and viewing anything new with suspicion. In other words, we are now doing things that were worldly ten or twenty years ago!

Soaring eagles

The church doesn't need any more parrots, mimicking one another on their evangelical/charismatic perches, clinging to their outdated cages. It is not enough to be taught happy, new parrot phrases if we lose our ability to fly. We need daring, soaring eagles. Original thinkers whose aim is to serve God and his people. Men who will break out of the cage and fly from religious captivity into the morality and purposes of God.

God is looking for a people who will find fresh and creative ways of communicating the gospel, outside of the cloistered emphasis of church meetings, buildings and para-church organizations. Men and women unafraid to be among the first to think, say and do things which are radical and prophetic. Not extra-scriptural in the sense of truth being added to—if such a thing were possible. But to bring out of our lifestyles things 'old and new' through which God would wish to speak to those around us. Prophets will always speak truth that is relevant to their specific cultural and moral situation.

Tragically, however, even some of those who sound like eagles, on closer inspection live like parrots. One man I know of spoke out strongly against his denominational structure, leadership and Bible college. He then joined the Bible college, fed the denomination with academic geniuses, thus furthering and supporting the very thing he spoke against—killing the church by degrees! It is hopeless declaring the need for soaring eagles on the one hand while fastening padlocks to the cage doors on the other.

Universal faith—local culture

God's people have been given a great measure of freedom to form their worship and corporate identity in a way that best suits their cultural and historical situation. How absurd, for example, to have the Southern Baptists in Tokyo or the Anglican Church in South Africa! The missionary work of God should never be frustrated, slowed down or diverted by loyalty to an unscriptural calendar, overseas headquarters or imposed statements of faith. Superstitious reverence for religious men, religious days and religious places must go. True religion is found in Jesus, not in our cultural hang-ups from the past, never mind those of other nations. Religious temples, shrines and mountains are reserved for other faiths, binding their worshippers to a static view of culture. We have exported the seeds of western cultural Christianity and we have for the last two or three decades been reaping the rewards of our folly, as many of our missionary efforts have been rejected.

When we ignore our cultural limitations, or when we impose those limitations on other nations, the gospel is bound to be hindered. Each nation must be left free to work out the morality of God within their own culture according to the general tenure of Scripture.

For example, in some Latin countries, two laughing, talking men walking arm in arm through a main street is an expression of warmth, friendship and trust. Two men doing the same thing in most high streets in Britain would create quite a different response! In meetings we are quite free, and it is often appropriate to hold hands while praying or to put arms round one another while singing, counselling or talking to one another. However, in the high street it is inappropriate. The gospel is not to be confused with homosexual activity.

Disqualified

Denominations, fellowships and organizations who unite on the basis of specific teachings (Sunday observance, teetotalism, inflexible forms of worship, clergy/laity distinctions) disqualify themselves as being Christ's universal faith for all cultures. It is quite in order to favour specific forms of leadership, worship or lifestyle in certain circumstances. It is another thing altogether when that form is imposed on a national or international network irrespective of local culture.

In order to honour God in our changing environment, we have continually to re-examine our position, even the most up-to-date. Otherwise we may find we are endeavouring to honour God in a way he has never required. Like my son who thought he was doing me a favour by weeding the garden. He also pulled out half my plants! His heart attitude was good, but he was also very destructive!

Only Jesus is free from all sin, error and deception. Our salvation and shared life must not rest in our apparent sinlessness or doctrinal and behavioural likemindedness. Many Christians have split from the mainline denominations as a protest against the church tolerating sin and covering it up, defending a course of fossilization and sterile worship. But as usually happens, in the second or third generation those new forms have in their turn become fixed cultures and traditions. They became institutionalized, and so we are back to square one. We need a motto that says, 'Constant change is here to stay,' and then we must go out and live it.

Scaffolding or building?

Most of the things I listed in the first paragraph of this chapter have got nothing to do with what God is building. They all have to do with the scaffolding. Scaffolding is used in order to get something built. The tragedy among many believers is simply that they are convinced that the scaffolding *is* the building! Take away clergy, buildings, Sunday schools, conferences, choirs and para-church organizations and what is left? In most localities precious little. But all of those things are mere scaffolding to get the building erected. The building is made up of living stones built into God and one another, continually growing, making room for that growth. Even the Bible is a form of scaffolding, inasmuch as it is God's provision from now until the age to come, but does not go to make up the final building—a redeemed people.

But today we have gold-plated scaffolding, ecclesiastical scaffolding, new radical scaffolding. Much of church life is simply a comparison between our scaffolding and that of others. Who's got the best scaffolding? But scaffolding in the trade is simply called 'temporary works'. Our problem is that we have made them permanent!

Is it any wonder that the world cannot see what is being built because of the conglomeration of scaffolding that surrounds the building? Is it any surprise that the world does not understand our gospel when it is crowded round with tubing, tarpaulin and activity? All they see of God's people are the same old crowd doing the same old things in the same old buildings in the same old way—with the same old result! They see it on TV too. The Sunday God-slot has probably done more damage to the nation's view of God and his people than anything else I can think of that has appeared on television.

We will have to learn, as the Jews did of old, that even if

God allows a temple, he will eventually destroy it if it comes between him and his people. So today. If God finds that things he once allowed are coming between him and his people, he will certainly demolish them and cast them aside like idols.

Frustrated in your local?

The proposals I have put forward may seem radical. In fact they are not. They all have to do with the scaffolding and not the building—scaffolding that has now mostly outlived its usefulness and is in danger of collapsing pretty soon anyway. Following my recommendations would only clear the way for us to see what we are building and for the world to see what God is doing.

I have heard it said that what happened to Samson can be likened to what God is doing within institutional Christianity. He may have lost his power, but his hair grew back again. I think this analogy is highly suspect. We need to ask ourselves, has God anointed and commissioned the institutional church (as against the rest of the church) to do what Samson did? If the answer is either 'questionable', or 'no', then the analogy fails.

To my mind, if a denominational church has a thorough and ongoing renewal, then everything is open to change except the truth. If that is the case, then our existing leadership, structures and traditions are not only open to change by renewal, but they are open to being dispensed with altogether, especially if they are no longer a suitable administration for God's purposes. A thoroughly renewed Anglican church minus its building, prayer book and dog-collared clergy would cease to be an Anglican church! A Pentecostal Assembly which has grown out of its building, broken down into cell groups, with shared leadership, no longer wanting to bang the denominational drum, will cease to be denominationally minded. It will just end up as a part of the church in that locality.

There is one very important fact, however, that we need to be aware of: successful and thorough ongoing renewal, reformation and restoration do not start at grass-roots level. They start at leadership level.

A minister or elder pulled all ways by the factions within his congregation may eventually collapse with a nervous breakdown. He cannot be a traditionalist, radical, Calvinist, charismatic, and conservative evangelical all at the same time! There may be grass-root-level renewal going on in his congregation, but unless he is leading it, there is bound to be an explosion.

Many have stayed within their denominational situations because they are praying for the 'minister' to become a Christian. A very commendable thing to do, but generally such action is not thought through. In other circumstances, we would never pray for an unbeliever at our factory or business and see him come through to Christ, only to put him in charge of our church straight away! Especially when others may have been converted ten or fifteen years and be much more mature. But this is precisely what is expected in many institutional church situations.

A group of evangelical believers begin to pray for their minister. Eventually, through answer to prayer, God graciously visits him with salvation and he is wonderfully filled with the Spirit. Officially he is leading them during the Sunday morning services, church meetings, etc. But in reality, they are leading him, because if it were not for them, their lives, their insight and understanding, he would not even be a Christian. And without them he would not grow in the way that God had intended. So we have a totally unreal situation which is extremely difficult, if not impossible, to put right.

What is the church?

There is a lot of talk these days about 'mixed congregations'. Such language and theology is foreign to the Bible. The church can no more be made up of unregenerate unbelievers indulging in the more acceptable sins of humanity, than the Boy Scouts can be made up of Bunny Girls!

To break bread or take communion with rows of people who you know have no living relationship with Jesus, is tantamount to hypocrisy and should not be found among the people belonging to a holy, creative, redeeming God.

A friend of mine took me out for supper in London one evening while I was writing this final chapter of the book. I explained that our community had been something of a cruise liner, with a somewhat damaged, sick, war-weary crew. After several years God now had an army of healthy people, and he was giving us a re-fit. We sensed he was equipping us to be a battleship. Before I could explain any further he quipped, 'Well, Gerald, my church is neither of those.' He raised his eyebrows, grinned and declared, 'Ours is like a rowing boat going round in circles with one oar missing!'

Within denominational Christianity there are many fine examples of a community seeking to honour God and one another. They are preaching and teaching the gospel, seeking to allow that gospel to affect every area of their lifestyle. But it has to be said that, even amidst the current renewal, they are exceptions to the rule. Most are like my friend's rowing boat!

To stay or not to stay...

God is growing fresh, new, green pastures. It is historically true that movements that have most recently known blessing in the past generally oppose the new blessing which is moving out into new pastures. This is especially true if the new pastures threaten the livelihood of the old! The new of course is more attractive and no doubt there is a lot of immature behaviour when fresh new fields are found. But perhaps a lot of it is not so much immaturity as relief and excitement—the new hope that comes with fresh discovery.

The old order, generally speaking, doesn't like the new. The Pharisees came into conflict with Jesus over this very issue. They emerged in Ezra's time, responding well to God's call to deal with the evils that had gained acceptance during Israel's period of captivity. When they returned to their promised land, a new order began to be established. They became known as the 'separated ones' because of their devotion to God's ways. Inevitably they experienced wonderful blessing from the hand of God. But, as is usual when God blesses a group, they ended up feeling that theirs was the only way of doing things, or at least far superior to everyone else's. Eventually these attitudes led their followers into legalism to the minutest detail and letter of the law. They ended up living by the rules instead of life, using their minds rather than their hearts on all religious matters. Eventually they opposed *anything* that didn't fit in with their already tried, proven and blessed past.

So it is not a matter of 'stay in' or 'come out' of a church denomination. It is a matter of *move on* or *go back*! Each of us must interpret what moving on or going back means, for we will be held accountable to God. We need have no doubt about that. We may deceive ourselves and others, but we cannot deceive the One who knows the hearts of men through and through. Even 'standing still' means going back—because God is moving on!

If God is growing fresh new grass you can't expect the

sheep to put up with a meagre diet, lacking in sustenance and nutrition, denied the very things that God intends. You can't blame the sheep for wanting to go under, over or through a barrier when their lives are at risk and hope is offered elsewhere, and there is of course a world of difference between a pen and pasture land.

Then there is a further cause of frustration. The things once criticized and rejected—such as new worship songs, raising hands, house groups, community, certain gifts of the Holy Spirit—can be tacked on and applauded as 'acceptable' while the basic attitude of the church remains unaffected. Such attempts at providing an answer can only be likened to rearranging the deckchairs on the *Titanic*, for all the good it will eventually do.

Of course, if a church is really dead it doesn't need new forms in which to express itself! Tarting up the church coffin will not produce a resurrection. That is why the ecumenical movement is such a hopeless disaster. Putting highly polished coffins together will not produce a resurrection community either. But if there is life—and there's loads of it within institutional Christianity—then with careful handling and encouragement it will find expression.

Radical recommendations?

So my 'mediocre recommendations' are not nearly as devastating as you may have supposed. They are merely superficial. All they will do is help us assess where we really are in terms of being built into God and one another. Instead of God having to break into the structures, he will be able to break out of his people! Many of our dreams will become realities, and they will also become the devil's nightmare! About time!

We must pray that the current upheaval of blessing, challenges and doubts which we are facing will not become a mere footnote in history but the headlines! The existence of every individual who has been born of God's Spirit, every Christian community that is seeking to please the Lord Jesus, will be continually affirming and reaffirming the existence of the living God. Declaring in message and lifestyle what he is like without adding to the list of growing discrepancies that currently exist between word and deed.

No longer will the world have to cope with churchgoers who revere a Bible they do not truly believe in. Giving public politeness to leaders they hold in private contempt. Reciting a creed which by their daily expression they totally disregard. No more religious buildings filled with people who do not know God and have little spiritual awareness, living in a barren world of unreality where everything is controlled, timed and carried out with precision-like detail.

God wants a people, a kingdom people, who will be a prophetic voice to the nations. Declaring in word and deed that God is not complacent over the current state of those who claim to be his people. Those willing to go with God will have many sacrifices to make, loads to bear, tears to shed and criticisms to contend with. They will no longer wish to be ranked among the casualties of religious systems—they will want to be conquerors. Conquerors of the world's system and the religious system. A people among whom God's purposes will be expressed in their priorities.

Such a people are on the earth already, growing in number, in stature, in wisdom and power—they are kingdom people, people of the King. At the moment they live in shadows; but they shall live in the light—for ever!

A Final Word?

I said at the beginning of this book that it was not a theological exposition of the Scriptures regarding the kingdom of God. There are large areas I have felt unqualified to write about.

There is the issue of miracles. We've all seen miracles. Certainly I have. I've experienced them in my own body, in my church and ministry as I've prayed for others. And I believe that this kingdom as it emerges will be full of 'signs and wonders'. But I have left this subject to others who have more to write and say than I do at present.

Then there is the demanding area of social justice and care for those outside the kingdom. Here again I could fill many pages with testimony to what the Holy Spirit has led us to do in our own town in Cobham for those outside the kingdom. The sharing of our goods, finances, plain simple love and care. But to me these things are too new to us and to share them prematurely would I think be unwise.

I have had to live with the fact that within this book there are many blurred edges, loose ends and unanswered questions. I wish it were different, for I have the normal human desire to define things, to tie up ends and answer all the questions. By God's grace I've resisted the temptation to write 'filler' chapters to sew everything up into a nice, neat package. I am conscious that I still have much to learn and so if God permits there will be more later.

In the meantime, let's press on together to discover creatively all that the gospel sets us free to embrace. While we seek to walk in the morality of our living God, let us push back the boundaries with our faith firmly rooted in Jesus. Let us be part of that 'many-membered' corporate man, showing by our words and our lives what it is to bring in God's kingdom on the earth.

The Words of Jesus

All scriptures are from the New International Version.

But seek first his kingdom and his righteousness, and all these things will be given to you as well.

Matthew 6:33

Anyone who breaks one of the least of these commandments and teaches others to do the same will be called least in the kingdom of heaven, but whoever practises and teaches these commands will be called great in the kingdom of heaven.

Matthew 5:19

Not everyone who says to me, 'Lord, Lord,' will enter the kingdom of heaven, but only he who does the will of my Father who is in heaven.

Matthew 7:21

Then the righteous will shine like the sun in the kingdom of their Father.

Matthew 13:43

The kingdom of heaven is like treasure hidden in a field. When a man found it, he hid it again, and then in his joy went and sold all he had and bought that field.

Matthew 13:44

Again I tell you, it is easier for a camel to go through the eye of a needle than for a rich man to enter the kingdom of God.

Matthew 19:24

I tell you the truth, the tax collectors and the prostitutes are entering the kingdom of God ahead of you.

Matthew 21:31

Come, you who are blessed by my Father; take your inheritance, the kingdom prepared for you since the creation of the world.

Matthew 25:34

The time has come.... The kingdom of God is near. Repent and believe the good news!

Mark 1:15

I tell you the truth, anyone who will not receive the kingdom of God like a little child will never enter it.

Mark 10:15

Blessed are you who are poor, for yours is the kingdom of God.

Luke 6:20

Do not be afraid, little flock, for your Father has been pleased to give you the kingdom. Sell your possessions and give to the poor. Provide purses for yourselves that will not wear out, a treasure in heaven that will not be exhausted, where no thief comes near and no moth destroys. For where your treasure is, there your heart will be also.

Luke 12:32–34

The kingdom of God does not come visibly, nor will people say, 'Here it is,' or 'There it is,' because the kingdom of God is within you.

Luke 17:20–21

Unless a man is born again, he cannot see the kingdom of God.

John 3:3

Pioneer Enterprises

Pioneer Bulletin, a quarterly publication which will keep you in touch with Gerald's ministry, is available by written request.

The bulletin carries a major article of topical interest by Gerald, along with details of events he is involved with. A list of his literature, audio and video tapes, plus new releases, is carried in each issue. Also covered are details of where donated money is being invested, in developing countries and evangelistic situations.

Pioneer Bulletin is not available in the shops, and can only be received by writing to Pioneer Enterprises, P.O. Box 80, Cobham, Surrey KT11 2BQ. There is no charge for *Pioneer Bulletin,* and it will be sent free if requested. However, donations are extremely welcome and cheques should be made out to Pioneer Enterprises. Send a stamped addressed envelope and you will receive a leaflet explaining how you can subscribe as an individual or on behalf of your group.

The Radical Christian

by Arthur Wallis

God's Holy Spirit is at work to change us into the likeness of Christ. Do we realize what a radical change this means?

This book challenges us to re-examine some of our cherished customs and beliefs. It shows how Scripture can guide us over such issues as church unity, water and Spirit baptism, and denominational loyalty.

The author confesses that this has not been an easy book to write. Nor will it be easy for us to receive. It calls for a verdict on God's truth— and so for a verdict on ourselves. Each one of us must decide: am I a compromiser, or a radical?

The axe is laid to the root of the tree.

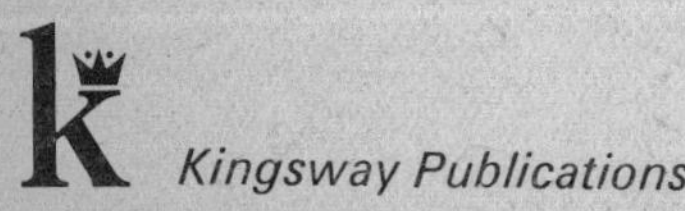

Built to Last

by Ron Trudinger

When Ron Trudinger wrote *Cells for Life* many churches were discovering the advantages of subdividing into home groups.

Since then a sequel has become necessary, because there is a real danger of introducing home groups as little more than a church face-lift. If the principles underlying church restoration are not understood, there will be no lasting benefit for the church. 'Restoration' is the necessary return to clear biblical patterns of church structure.

In this book Ron Trudinger (a pastor at Basingstoke Community Church) draws on his experience of restoration church life to apply the Bible's teaching in a direct and practical way.

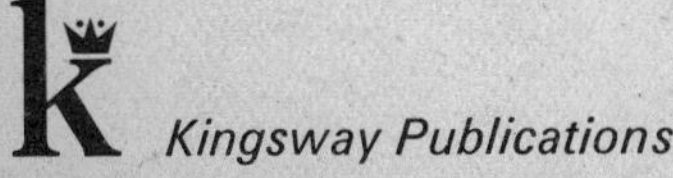